THE CASTLE LECTURES IN ETHICS,

POLITICS, AND ECONOMICS

The Hidden Face of Rights

Toward a Politics of Responsibilities

KATHRYN SIKKINK

Yale

UNIVERSITY PRESS

New Haven and London

Yale University Press books may be purchased in quantity for educational, business, or promotional use. For information, please e-mail sales.press@yale.edu (U.S. office) or sales@yaleup.co.uk (U.K. office).

Set in Janson and Monotype Van Dijck types by IDS Infotech Ltd.
Printed in the United States of America.

Library of Congress Control Number: 2019946785
ISBN 978-0-300-23329-2 (hardcover : alk. paper)

A catalogue record for this book is available from the British Library.

This paper meets the requirements of ANSI/NISO Z39.48-1992 (Permanence of Paper).

10 9 8 7 6 5 4 3 2 1

Parts of this book were given as the Castle Lectures in Yale's Program in Ethics, Politics, and Economics, delivered by Kathryn Sikkink in 2017.

The Castle Lectures were endowed by Mr. John K. Castle. They honor his ancestor the Reverend James Pierpont, one of Yale's original founders. Given by established public figures, Castle Lectures are intended to promote reflection on the moral foundations of society and government and to enhance understanding of ethical issues facing individuals in our complex modern society.

To the memory of my father, Donald Sikkink (1928–2018),
and to my mother, Arlene Angel Sikkink

Contents

Preface: In Memory

This book is dedicated to the memory of my father, who died while I was writing it, and to my mother, still vividly alive. They were the first to teach me about rights. As a girl, I listened to my mother arguing for women's rights and my father defending the right to free speech for unpopular beliefs. Later, I learned about the rights of distant others when I saw my parents protesting the Vietnam War.

My father taught speech and communication at a state college in a conservative midwestern town. When he retired, he endowed a small library and speaker fund in his department. The revenue generated from this fund supports one or more speakers every year, with a preference for those who, in my father's words, would "be in jail were it not for the First Amendment."

My parents also modeled the responsibilities that accompany rights, including the responsibility to vote; the responsibility to pay taxes; and the responsibilities to speak out, to protest, and to listen to the speech of others. While I visited my parents in Tucson in March 2017, three generations of my family sat down together to write postcards to the White House, asking President Donald Trump to release his tax returns. My parents (in their late eighties), my son (twenty-four), and my husband and I all had been working on our tax returns in the previous week. I was raised to think of paying taxes as a civic duty—something we owed to society in return for the public schools where everyone in my family studied, good roads and bridges, police and fire protection, and other state services, including services for those less fortunate than ourselves. In Minnesota, where I grew up and where good state and local governance was a matter of work and pride, it did not seem old-fashioned or naïve to think we had a responsibility to pay taxes.

My father also felt strongly about political leaders' responsibility to be transparent about their finances. He asked my sister to make him a T-shirt saying, "Voters deserve six years of tax returns from all candidates"; he often wore it in his Arizona retirement community, where many didn't share his views. This was not unusual. My dad was known for his political T-shirts. My favorite showed a bear carrying a gun, above the words, "I support the right to arm bears."

What most worried us was not that Trump refused to release his tax returns. It was that he thought avoiding taxes was clever, and he took pride in it. During the campaign, when some pointed out that he had paid no federal income tax for years, he said, "That makes me smart." I wasn't brought up to think that not paying taxes makes one smart.

As my research began to engage more with the simultaneous need to stress both rights and responsibilities, my parents' lessons often came to mind. Watching our presidential elections and hearing that, consistently, more U.S. citizens did not vote than voted for either of the major parties' candidates, I wondered what was happening to our collective sense of a civic duty to vote. In an age of increasing gun violence, gun owners stressed their right to bear arms with little discussion of the responsibilities that must accompany such a right. The haste to reform U.S. tax laws seemed to arise from a complete absence of a sense of civic responsibility to pay taxes in order to make possible policies that would benefit the most disadvantaged. The defense of the legitimate and important right to practice one's religion was being made without consideration of the equally important responsibility not to discriminate against others based on, for example, their sexual orientation. I began to realize that rights are incomplete unless accompanied by a deep sense of responsibilities.

But as I started to talk about these ways to combine rights and responsibilities, I began to encounter all sorts of unusual opposition—not from opponents of rights but from rights advocates. This resistance puzzled me and increased my sense that the topic deserved exploration.

I soon learned that the very words *duty*, *responsibility*, and *obligation* put people off. They have become associated with a narrow and punitive definition of personal responsibility in the context of individual welfare. In addition, the ordinary meanings as well as the legal meanings of duty and responsibility involve accountability, liability, and blame. No matter how it is said, responsibility implies "should," and people don't like being told what they should do.

Following Iris Marion Young's lead from her book *Responsibility for Justice*, I stress a forward-looking responsibility based not on blame but on what she has called "a social connection model" and what I will call "networked responsibility," where all the people and institutions who are connected to injustice are called upon to act in concert to address these problems. Let's think of it not as "Who is to blame?" but as what together we can do to implement human rights in the world. Conceived in this way, responsibility is empowering. Continuing to fashion a better world requires us to stress rights in the fullest sense and to stress the responsibilities of multiple actors to take action to fulfill these rights.

Acknowledgments

First and foremost, I want to thank Fernando Berdion del Valle for encouraging me to explore these issues with him in our coauthored article, which has informed my thinking, and for his permission to use some material from that article in this book. I have so many colleagues, students, and friends to thank for their help, support, comments, or questions that I fear I cannot do justice to all of them. I am particularly grateful to William Clark, Dara Cohen, Jenny Mansbridge, Martha Minow, Joseph Nye, and Mathias Risse for close readings and detailed comments and suggestions on chapters of the book. Stephan Parmentier shared with me his own edited book on rights and responsibilities and reminded me of a less well-known sentence of John Kennedy's 1961 Inaugural Address that I cite at the start of Chapter One. Nancy Thomas's help was fundamental to the entire discussion of student voting and free speech on campus, as was the work of Miles Rappaport and Archon Fung. Stephen Livingston helped me think about all issues involving technology, and Robert Keohane encouraged me to address responsibilities for climate change. Sally Kenney and Dara Cohen gave me excellent feedback on the discussion of campus sexual assault. I am indebted in particular to Vafa Ghazavi, who first recommended I read Iris Young's *Responsibility for Justice*. I thank Frances Rosenbluth for her confidence in me; Steven Smith for excellent suggestions of further reading; Harold Koh, Seyla Benhabib, and Ian Shapiro, who attended the lectures, for their excellent questions and suggestions, and in particular to Harold for arguing that a person does not have a right not to vote. Institutionally I'm grateful to the Radcliffe Institute for Advanced Study and the Harvard Kennedy School, the two places where the research and writing on this book germinated. Roshni Chakraborty, Hannah Ellery, Jessica Tueller, and Catherine Zheng were my intrepid and self-motivated undergraduate research assistants when I was a fellow at the Radcliffe Institute. They did more extensive and thoughtful research than I could even begin to fully incorporate into the book. Jessica and Roshni continued to work with me as genuine research partners in the production of the book. I'm not sure how I could have finished the book without their help. My neighbor Melissa Franklin gave me great advice on the importance of telling stories. My husband, Douglas Johnson, and my dear friends, Sue Bumagin, Nancy Gaschott, Paul Korn, Mark Ritchie, and Cheryl Thomas, discussed the topic with me and encouraged me to write this book even though they understood that it might be controversial. I thank the following colleagues and friends for their thoughts and stories, comments on presentations and chapters, recommendations of authors to read, and issues and arguments to stress: Jaqueline Bhabha, Eric Blumenson, Leonardo Castilho, Ramsey Champagne, Mary Dietz, Marshall Ganz, Isabella Garbin, Frances Hagopian, Andrew Hurrell, Patricia Illingworth, Margaret Keck, Alex Keyssar, Steven Levitsky, Scott Mainwaring, Francis Moore Lappé, Samuel Moyn, Pedro Pontual, Samantha Power, Cesar Rodriguez Garvito, William Schultz, Beth Simmons, Mariano Sánchez-Talanque, Stephen Waltz, Melissa Williams, Leah Wright Rigueur, and Ezgi Yıldız, I want to give a special thanks to the members of my book club, Ingunn Bjornson, Ann Colony, Sue Elfin, Deb Fox, and Danyel Logevall, who read the entire draft manuscript and offered such helpful comments. I am also indebted to two philosophers I have never met, François Ost and Sebastien van Drooghenbroeck, whose article "La responsibilidad como cara oculta de los derechos humanos" provided the inspiration for the title of this book.

My editor at Yale, William Frucht, suggested I take up this issue for the Castle Lectures and the book. He has been an engaged presence through the entire process of preparing the lectures and writing the book, asking probing questions, making suggestions, directing me to literature, and even doing a fabulous edit of the manuscript, for which I am deeply grateful.

CHAPTER ONE

What Together We Can Do

And so, my fellow Americans: ask not what your country can
do for you, but what you can do for your country. My fellow
citizens of the world: ask not what America will do for you,
but what together we can do for the freedom of man.
—John F. Kennedy

MOST Americans know the first sentence of this quote from
John Kennedy's Inaugural Address in 1961, but many of us
don't recognize the second sentence, in which a U.S. president spoke to "fellow citizens of the world" and urged us to
think of our collective responsibilities for human rights.

Human rights are threatened in much of the world today,
including the United States. Everywhere, people and organizations have stepped forward to try to protect those rights. Yet the
discourse of human rights often omits the language of political
and ethical responsibilities, and that absence constrains the effectiveness of rights movements. We who believe in human
rights need to begin talking and thinking explicitly about the
politics and ethics of responsibility. A rights-and-responsibilities

approach is a framework, not a recipe for action. It requires us to think strategically about the networked responsibilities of many state and non-state actors, including individuals, to work collectively to implement human rights. There are risks and discomforts in emphasizing responsibilities, but the risks of inaction and complacency are worse.[1]

In 2018, we celebrated the seventieth anniversaries of the Universal Declaration of Human Rights (UDHR) and the American Declaration of the Rights and Duties of Man, a Latin American declaration that preceded the UDHR by eight months. Impressive work has gone into constructing an elaborate structure of rights in the past seventy years, but the huge gap in implementation between the ideals in human rights law and the realities on the ground has created disillusionment and despair. One way that those engaged in human rights work can begin to address this gap is to forge deeper links between rights and the diverse actors who bear responsibilities for their fulfillment. This project is already well under way, but somehow the norms and explicit strategizing around responsibility haven't caught up with practice.

Above all, the human rights approach stresses the responsibilities of states to fulfill rights. But states are often unwilling or unable to meet these obligations on their own. In some cases, it is impossible for human rights ideals to be reached without cooperation from other agents. Following Onora O'Neill, I will call these other actors "agents of justice."[2] Many potential agents of justice exist; they include international organizations, corporations, non-governmental organizations, social movements, universities, and individuals. Some are already fighting for justice, yet scholars and activists

have not found ways to talk about these networked obligations to fulfill rights.[3] I include myself in that category. I have
worked on human rights off and on for almost four decades,
yet until I started this project, my writing included few discussions of responsibility and none of duty.[4]

In this book, I will mainly *not* use the common legal meaning of *responsibility*, which focuses on who is accountable or
liable. This is what Iris Young has called "backward-looking
responsibility" or the "liability model of responsibility."[5] Instead I will focus on ethical and political responsibility that is
forward-looking. Forward-looking responsibilities are held by
states and corporations as well as by non-state institutions and
individuals, who are not necessarily liable or to blame for a
common human rights problem but can nevertheless help address it. This type of responsibility asks not "Who is to blame"
but "What should we do?"[6] It is aimed at accomplishing things
effectively rather than punishing those who are at fault.[7]
The forward-looking responsibilities I discuss in this book are
necessary to promote a broad range of civil, political, economic, and social rights.

I find it puzzling that so many human rights advocates
avoid talking about non-state responsibility because they are
among the people most driven by a deeply felt sense of personal responsibility. These activists may see human rights as a
cause or a calling rather than a responsibility. Yet in the 1970s
and 1980s, many members of the human rights movement
took their responsibilities to defend the rights of others so
seriously that human rights organizations were notorious for
not respecting the labor rights of their staff—such as the forty-
hour work week, a living wage, and regular paid vacations.

Some human rights workers suffer vicarious trauma from spending so much time listening to and sympathizing with victims of human rights violations. Fortunately, human rights organizations have become aware of the need to respect labor rights and provide psychological services to their members, but it remains true that many human rights workers feel so deeply their responsibility to work on behalf of others that they sometimes imperil their own health.[8]

Although activists may feel deeply about responsibility, they don't always like to talk about it. This could be a strategic framing choice by savvy activists because talking about rights is more compelling than reminding people of responsibilities. But the discomfort activists often express about responsibilities suggests there is something deeper at work. A friend of mine, Paul Korn, who is retired and devotes considerable time to volunteer work, told me that for him, "Responsibility is like breathing. I felt duty-bound [to take action], but I never used the word 'responsibility'; I never had the consciousness to think about it in those terms." He added, "When people are on the fence, you have to lead by example, not by preaching duty. And if I did try, people might say to me, 'Who are you to tell me what to do?'"[9] It is common to hear such comments from human rights activists; although they feel a deep personal responsibility to defend rights, they are uncomfortable "preaching" about responsibility to others. This is not an issue only for activists. Two of my most valued colleagues at the Harvard Kennedy School encouraged me to think about these issues.[10]

In other words, diverse human rights actors already have robust responsibility *practices*, yet we do not articulate clear *norms* in talking about our personal beliefs about responsibility to motivate a wider range of actors. In fact, the norms appear to require that one *not* talk about the responsibility of a wider range of actors because such talk might take the pressure off the state, risk blaming the victim, underplay the structural causes of injustice, or crowd out other more collective forms of political action. In this sense, diverse responsibilities are the hidden face of rights, present in the practices of human rights actors, but something that activists don't talk about. But I believe norms about wider responsibility practices among diverse actors, especially for rights with decentralized compliance decisions, are necessary to more fully implement these rights. In this book I will argue the following:

- To address environmental crises, it is necessary to emphasize not only our rights to a clean environment, but also the obligations of states, corporations, institutions, and individuals to protect the environment. Although much attention has correctly focused on the need for states and corporations to limit emissions in order to slow climate change, other institutions and individuals must complement state and corporate actions by working to decrease their own carbon footprints.

- To protect digital privacy and combat digital disinformation, we must demand that our government do more. But unless other organizations—especially corporations like Facebook and Google—take action, implementation will be radically incomplete. There is also a role for schools, universities, and individuals to step up digital training so that individuals can take actions to enhance their own privacy and help prevent the spread of disinformation. Unless individuals also take action to forward, retweet, or post material only from trustworthy sources, we will never be able to diminish the spread of so-called "fake news."

- To strengthen our political system, it is not enough to stress our right to vote; we also need to practice our responsibility to vote and to help others vote. Voter suppression is a conscious and well-orchestrated set of policies in many states; collective voter encouragement must be no less conscious. This is (or should be) the work of government and political parties, but especially in the present climate, it cannot be left only to them. All of us have responsibilities not only to vote, but also to help others exercise their legal right and responsibility to vote.

- To confront economic inequality, it is necessary to stress both the economic rights of individuals to an adequate standard of living and the duties of corporations and individuals to pay taxes so that their governments can combat poverty at home and abroad.[11] Our tax system would not function if it needed sanctions and audits to collect every dollar. Instead, it relies on norms about the responsibility to pay taxes.

- We need to protect our right to free speech and protest not only by exercising it, but also by practicing the responsibility not to drown out the speech of others.

For each of these issues, even if the state were to completely fulfill its responsibilities under human rights law, the rights still could not be fully implemented unless other actors stepped forward and did their share. The state can and should use incentives or sanctions to compel responsibility, but these are costly and crude tools. The voluntary acceptance of mutual responsibilities by a variety of actors is the key to full implementation of rights. Such voluntary acceptance comes via norms about appropriate behavior, not from fear of sanctions.

I can illustrate this statement with a recent example about the right to digital privacy. Many people once argued that they did not care about digital privacy because they had nothing to hide. The scandal in 2018 concerning Cambridge Analytica's misuse of Facebook data showed that people who were careless about their own privacy could endanger the privacy of millions of others. The two hundred thousand individuals who filled out surveys and inadvertently downloaded apps gave away information about their families, friends, and other contacts when the apps scraped the Facebook accounts of approximately eighty-seven million other users.

In the wake of this scandal, I wrote an op-ed, entitled "Wake Up, Hapless Technology Users," about networked responsibilities to protect digital privacy, including the responsibilities of individuals.[12] I recognized the failures of corporations and governments to protect our privacy, but I also noted that any discussion of an individual responsibility to protect digital privacy seemed to be absent from the debate. Individuals were portrayed as hapless and innocent victims of greedy corporations and indifferent governments, not as agents with the ability to take precautions against privacy violations.

In fact, I argued, technology users are not clueless victims but bearers of responsibilities, even if these are much smaller than the obligations of governments and corporations. I included myself as one of the hapless technology users who had not lived up to these responsibilities. When I read the story about Cambridge Analytica, I decided for the first time to check the privacy settings on my smartphone, only to discover that it had been cheerfully broadcasting my data to anyone who might be interested, even though options have long existed for me to block part of that access.

We should know by now that our smartphones are little spy machines that we carry around in our pockets, and our Facebook pages are open invitations for privacy violations. They are usually benevolent spy machines and certainly indispensable ones. Apple and Facebook tell us that the main reason for the spying is to curate marketing messages to meet our material needs more efficiently. But they are spy machines nonetheless, and this benevolent view can rapidly degrade into manipulation and abuse at the hands of unscrupulous, self-interested, and insufficiently regulated political and economic actors. Even if we do not care about our own privacy, the Cambridge Analytica scandal has made clear that when we neglect our responsibility to protect our own privacy, we leave our friends and contacts vulnerable.

Not surprisingly, corporations that receive a large part of their income from selling our data do not make it easy to block their ability to profit from us. As one of my students pointed out, "If the product is free, you *are* the product." Ideally the smartphones and other technology would arrive from the factory with high privacy protections, just as cars arrive with seat belts. But the business model of these technology corporations depends on selling their customers' private information, so they will never voluntarily make it easy for us to protect our privacy. We should lobby our government for legislation to mandate privacy protections and to question this business model.[13] In the meantime, technology users can take action themselves.

I included in my op-ed article simple instructions that I had discovered to fix my own privacy settings on the technologies I use every day, including my smartphone, Facebook, Google, and Firefox. No sooner was the piece published than my neighbors and colleagues started asking me to help change their privacy settings. It became dinner table conversation with friends and colleagues. My sons found it hilarious that anyone would ask their notoriously technologically inept mother for advice. But of the over fifty phones I looked at in the following months—phones belonging mainly to my well-educated and conscientious colleagues, students, and friends—only one had its privacy settings set to the maximum available protection. Most were unknowingly sharing all their data. I was very happy when the *Washington Post* and other outlets began publishing far more complete and informative instructions about how technology users could exercise some agency to protect their privacy and that of their friends, families, and acquaintances.[14]

After I wrote the op-ed article, I realized that the problem of digital disinformation is equally important and even more dependent on the exercise of individual responsibility. While fake news has been with us for a long time, has recently accelerated, and will probably always be with us, individuals are deeply implicated in the spread of disinformation.[15] Much fake news is spread by individuals who thoughtlessly forward an email, retweet, or post an item on their Facebook page without checking its accuracy. As such, individuals can take important actions to diminish the spread of disinformation, using the same skills that educators try to teach their students in the classroom: learning how to find, check, and share only trustworthy sources of information.

Having multiple obligation bearers in this case is crucial because privacy is a complex issue with decentralized compliance. Even if governments take action, the actual implementation needs to come from multiple actors, especially corporations. Corporations are unlikely to take action unless legally required by governments or unless it affects their bottom line. In the current political climate in the United States, our government is unlikely to step up to provide more protection for our online privacy rights. Until Facebook encounters determined government or consumer pressure—in the form of either more regulation, organized boycotts, or cancellations and suspensions of accounts—it may not respond appropriately. But Facebook, Apple, Google, and even Amazon hold us hostage. We are so dependent on our accounts with these companies that the cost of cancelling them feels too great.

I am writing this book for people like the readers of my op-ed article who asked for help: people who are willing to take responsibility but who feel too busy to take action. I am writing for people like my friend Paul, already working for social justice but not yet thinking explicitly in terms of responsibility, and for human rights students and scholars who, perhaps like me, were raised to think about responsibility *and* rights but do not feel empowered to talk about the responsibility part of the equation.

I will be making a political and ethical argument, not a legal argument that we should change human rights law to make obligations binding. I will not propose that we revise our human rights treaties to add in responsibilities! Mine is a political argument in the sense stressed by theorists like Hannah Arendt and Iris Marion Young (whose influence I discuss more fully in chapter 3) because it involves debating and working with others collectively to incorporate responsibilities explicitly when we promote human rights and oppose structural injustices.[16] In this sense, I draw on Arendt and Young to think about "what together we can do," to echo the Kennedy quote cited on the first page of this chapter.

Some progressive writers and activists are so focused on rights that rather than speak of responsibilities, they bend over backward to frame issues as rights claims. For example, environmental activists have increasingly started to speak of our right to a clean environment, the rights of trees, the rights of the rivers, and the rights of Mother Earth herself, as reflected in the Pachamama laws of Bolivia and Ecuador.[17] An environmental group has brought a lawsuit to give the Colorado River legal rights.[18] If it succeeds, that river will join a small handful of others, such as the Ganges, that have legal rights.[19] While I am not opposed to rivers, trees, or even Mother Earth having rights, I think it is also necessary to stress the responsibilities of countries, corporations, states and municipalities, organizations, and individuals to protect them.

My purpose is not to argue against rights as an approach to addressing environmental or any other issues. I am impressed by efforts to protect future generations' rights to a safe environment. But once we realize that future generations have this right, we also know that it is insufficient to insist that only states or corporations have responsibilities. All of us connected to the structural injustice of climate change need to exercise our collective responsibilities. In order to fulfill and enjoy rights, we need increased attention to the responsibilities of diverse actors.

One barrier to getting people to assume responsibilities for issues like a clean environment is the classic problem of collective action and large numbers. People hope that others will take action and they can free ride. Overcoming free riding is always difficult, but it is especially difficult when individual actions are minuscule in their effects. This is also a problem in voting behavior (discussed below), where economists have long argued that voting is irrational: the cost of one person going to the poll is greater than the benefit one additional vote adds to the outcome. People may feel that anything they do is a mere drop in the ocean, so why should they act at all? In order to overcome these problems, it will be important to stress the intrinsic satisfaction we get by carrying out responsibilities. In other words, to encourage people to assume responsibilities, we need to think of how to mobilize the full range of human emotions and motivations, including altruism and a sense of satisfaction one gets from performing civic responsibilities, and not just the pursuit of narrow self-interest.[20]

There are some conditions under which networked obligations are particularly essential for protecting rights. Complex and new rights issues, such as climate change and digital privacy, for which compliance decisions are decentralized, are especially in need of networked obligations of multiple agents of justice.[21] This distinction between rights with decentralized or centralized compliance decisions is not common in the literature, so it may be useful to explain exactly what I mean.

There are some rights issues where government action alone can lead to the implementation of rights. The right to be free from capital punishment, for example, depends on decisions made in the top levels of government. This is a centralized compliance decision. If a state legislature votes to end capital punishment in that state, or if the U.S. Supreme Court decides that capital punishment is a violation of the constitutional protection against cruel and unusual punishment, these actions are sufficient to implement the right within the relevant jurisdiction.[22] The compliance decisions about other rights, meanwhile, are highly decentralized—for instance, women's rights to be safe from violence—and are more difficult to implement. In the case of women's rights, the state can (and should) pass laws and adopt policies that give women more protection, including, for example, making it easier for victims of violence to obtain restraining orders. But the actual compliance decision is often made by individuals in a household, a workplace, or a university. State compliance is necessary but not at all sufficient to address sexual assault, for example, and a wider range of networked actors must take responsibility to end violent practices. I will return to this topic in the final chapter of this book.

One advantage of a decentralized compliance decision is that even when the national government is unwilling or unable to take action, other levels of government, as well as non-state institutions, corporations, and individuals, can still work toward implementation. The Trump administration in the United States, for example, has withdrawn from the Paris Agreement on climate change and refused to comply with international environmental standards to limit climate change. Nevertheless, various state governments, municipal governments, corporations, universities, and individuals in the United States have affirmed their commitment to the agreement and to continue to diminish carbon emissions despite the federal government's noncompliance.

The examples I use to illustrate my argument (and they are only illustrative, not full-fledged case studies) all involve such decentralized issues. In chapter 3, I will discuss climate change and privacy and disinformation in the digital world more in depth; in chapters 4, 5, and 6, I will take up the rights and responsibilities to vote; and in chapter 7, I will discuss protections for protest and free speech and the problem of sexual assault on campus.

So why is an international relations scholar writing a book about human rights and responsibilities, with long sections on new rights like the right to a clean environment and digital privacy, the right and responsibility to vote in the United States, and the rights and responsibilities on college campuses for speech and protest as well as around issues of sexual assault? Some of this is new territory for me. Why am I going there?

As a scholar of democracy and human rights, I am interested in the way social change occurs, globally and in the United States, over long periods of time, and the role that changes in norms, ideas, and practices play in those processes.

In my previous work, I have traced the history of norms and networks that have reshaped our world, and some of these insights are as relevant for talking about rights and responsibilities in the United States as they are for the global sphere. I am not a philosopher or a lawyer, and I will not advocate constructing new moral duties in an ideal world or new legal duties in this one. Instead, I will address the practical politics of norm construction. I will argue, for example, that we do not yet have strong and well-internalized norms in this country about the importance of voting, but it is possible to build norm campaigns for a responsibility to vote.

My previous research has taught me something about processes of norm construction and enforcement. When we talk about norm change, we mean changing our standards of appropriate behavior. I have studied the historical norm campaigns of anti-slavery and women's suffrage, as well as campaigns less known in the United States, such as the anti-foot-binding movement in China and campaigns against female genital cutting in Kenya. I have also written about campaigns for the creation of human rights declarations, for individual criminal accountability for mass atrocity, and for a global response to violence against women. Each of these campaigns began with the agency of individuals and groups in the face of what appeared to be insurmountable structural odds. I call these people norms entrepreneurs, reform mongers, or transnational advocacy networkers. They are driven by principles and strategy, working carefully to garner as much support as possible. Sometimes my more structuralist colleagues tell me it is a mistake to focus on the agency of norm entrepreneurs. For example, when I started researching the abolition of slavery, a colleague calmly informed me that slavery ended because it ceased to be profitable. But the more I researched it, the more it became clear, as the historian of slavery Robert Fogel has argued, that slavery was ended at the peak of its economic success by men and women "ablaze with moral fervor."[23] From my past work, I have come to believe in the necessity, the possibility, and the efficacy of individual and collective agency in bringing about normative and policy changes in systems and structure.

I have also learned about what Martha Finnemore and I call "the life cycle of norms."[24] In the first stage, principled and strategic actors help create and diffuse new norms. If these norms become widely accepted, they may be internalized in the hearts and minds of the broader population and grow to be taken for granted. At this point, people may adhere to norms not because they share a conviction but because that is simply the thing to do. In other words, people sometimes adhere to internalized norms in an expression of conformity rather than belief. One way we can identify a well-established norm is that norm breakers may receive social sanctions. If there were a strong norm in this country to vote, for example, people would ask others if they had voted and stigmatize them if they had not.

Well-internalized norms that are no longer much debated, but are accepted and perhaps even taken for granted, include, for example, women's right to vote. We no longer debate whether women should be permitted to vote (except in places like Saudi Arabia). In fact, we know this is a well-internalized norm because it is almost impossible to find someone disputing it. The only person I could find who questions female suffrage in the United States is alt-right leader Richard Spencer, who dreams of founding a patriarchal white ethnostate.[25]

As a "senior" scholar, I can tell you not only about my research on norms, but also about massive norm shifts I have witnessed in my lifetime. I remember a world where there were virtually no women professors, where many in LGBTI (Lesbian, Gay, Bixsexual, Transgender, Intersex) communities were afraid to discuss their sexual orientation even with close friends, and where I did not know what transgender meant. I remember a world where it was common to smoke anywhere one wanted to, including closed spaces with one's children; where parents did not put seat belts on their kids; where recycling bins did not exist; and where I would not have known the meaning of the term *designated driver*. I now live in a country where women account for approximately 40 percent of full-time faculty in political science departments; where LGBTI communities have won significant victories, including provisions for same-sex marriage; where debates over transgender issues are prominent; where most people buckle up; where smoking is prohibited widely; where 35 percent of waste is recycled; and where my sons and their friends take for granted that one of them will be the designated driver when they go out drinking. Government action and laws spurred many of these changes, but if we look closely at how they occurred, we often see that the early advocacy parts of the norm life cycle preceded the laws and contributed to them. The norm against smoking indoors had already started to emerge before the introduction of strong and extensive smoking bans. Adult smoking rates in the United States decreased markedly for both males and females from 1965 to 2001, but it was not until the late 1990s and early 2000s that some states implemented comprehensive smoking bans that prohibited smoking in most workplaces and all public places.[26] These bans in turn accelerated the process of norm change, so that by 2018 cigarette use among Americans had dropped to its lowest level ever recorded: 14 percent of the population now smokes, as compared to 60 percent in the mid-1960s.[27]

We could distinguish between norms, like those having to do with seat belts and smoking—where the self-interest of people is clear and the norm is just trying to get them to follow their self-interest—and norms that require people to promote the rights of others at no benefit to themselves. But anyone who has tried to quit smoking knows that it is not always easy to act in one's self-interest, and it may take both powerful social sanctions and laws to finally get one to act in one's own interest. Laws can play a useful educational or expressive role in norm change, but coercion is not always the best tool to bring about norm change. Often nudges and/or peer pressure are more helpful than fines or exhortation when it comes to norm change. As we will see in the chapters on voting, for example, the most important factors helping students to vote are the climate on campus and the voices of their peers and professors.

I do not have a simple view of norm shifts. Some people say there are good and bad norms, but since a norm is defined as a standard of appropriate behavior, there are always some who think the norm they advocate is good. It would be more correct to say that there are norms with which one agrees or disagrees. There are of course global norm campaigns with which I disagree, such as the ones to promote a global right to bear arms and to criminalize homosexuality. Among the norms I support, there are many campaigns that fail and other cases where norms we thought were well internalized can suffer dramatic backsliding. One example is the history of the use of torture by the United States. The norm against torture was almost universally accepted before 2001, but we have now fallen back to a position where U.S. officials and political candidates, including President Trump, not only accept it, but also publicly advocate it.

PUSHBACK AND CLARIFICATION

I have gotten a lot of pushback on these arguments, so a few clarifications are in order.

The most important is that not all human rights scholars and activists are reluctant to discuss the role of non-state political responsibilities, obligations, or duties to respect or ensure rights.[28] Many important philosophers, for example, have contributed to the understanding of individual duties and responsibilities as essential to the nature of rights and necessary for their fulfillment.[29] These philosophers argue that the very logic of rights-talk implies that for every right someone must be assigned the corresponding duty to help fulfill that right. We may disagree about how to assign such duties but not about their necessity.[30] Jeremy Waldron has taken this a step further and argued that certain rights are actually responsibilities.[31]

In his classic 1996 book, *Basic Rights*, Henry Shue elaborates the various types of moral duties of all actors that are necessary to contribute to the enjoyment of rights.[32] Charles Beitz writes of the "demand side" of human rights and also the "supply side," by which he means "the reason why some class of agents should regard themselves as under an obligation to respect or enforce the human rights of others." He distinguishes between the "first-level" responsibilities of states, with the primary duty to respect and protect rights, and the "second-level" responsibilities of other agents, who may need to act when governments cannot or will not perform their responsibility.[33] Mathias Risse understands human rights as "rights that are accompanied by responsibilities at the global level," but he recognizes that duties across borders are "notoriously underspecified." He argues, borrowing Beitz's categories, that his own approach to human rights is supply-side focused, making global responsibilities central.[34] Thomas Pogge has recently drawn attention to the duties of individuals, arguing that citizens of wealthy countries are implicated in global injustice through their active or passive support of oppressive political regimes. Pogge recognizes that citizens of industrialized nations have "negative" duties not to impose unjust systems on the world's poor.[35]

Despite the arguments offered by philosophers, however, both the law and the practical politics of rights continue to be demand-side; to the degree that they look at the supply side, they have focused almost entirely on state duties. It is not enough to provide philosophical justifications; we also have to confront the political and normative barriers to further discussion of non-state responsibilities in relation to rights. Some philosophers recognize these barriers. Two Belgian philosophers, for example, say that responsibilities are often treated as if they were the "hidden and shameful face" of human rights that have been frequently erased or repressed in practice.[36]

For most of the twentieth century, when people spoke of responsibility, they meant responsibility for others—what one could and should do for other people. In the United States today, however, some argue that our notion of responsibility has transformed from an obligation to assist others to a narrow and sometimes punitive responsibility of poor people to take care of themselves under a receding welfare state.[37] Many feel that the very term *responsibility* has become a way of blaming victims for their own misfortunes, and even when human rights proponents use the term, it carries that baggage.[38] In *The Age of Responsibility*, Yascha Mounk argues that progressive people have sometimes avoided victim-blaming by adopting a "no-responsibility" view. He argues that rather than refusing to use the word, we should instead "reclaim" the broader understanding of responsibility.[39] Other political theorists have made related arguments.[40] In this book, I will argue that the concept of responsibility has the potential to provoke a debate that is intensely relevant to human rights and, if taken seriously, to help ensure the enjoyment and implementation of rights.

Some arguments about responsibility understandably elicit caution from human rights scholars and activists. Some authors embrace responsibilities mainly to challenge rights, arguing that rights should be subject to limits and that these limits are defined by responsibilities.[41] Others claim that "rights talk" leads to the neglect of duties and stimulates the proliferation of questionable "rights," such as the right to peace or international solidarity.[42] States sometimes deny rights to individuals on the basis of the individuals' failure to perform certain duties. I completely reject the idea that rights and obligations should exist in some kind of legal conditional relationship that allows rights to be taken away if one does not comply with some responsibility. We have rights by virtue of being human, and they are not conditional on the performance of duties.

I frequently run into this misconception when I talk about reclaiming responsibility. When I published my *Boston Globe* op-ed article about the responsibilities of technology users, one of the first responses I received on Twitter said, in capital letters, "DON'T PUT THE BURDEN ON THE PEOPLE." I understand the concern that by pointing to individuals as having responsibilities, we may let governments and corporations off the hook. But I never suggested that people's privacy rights were contingent on their taking action or that states and corporations should not be held accountable. The "burden" I was placing on smartphone and Facebook users was that they take a few minutes to adjust the privacy settings on their own devices, software, and social media accounts.

I have also received pushback from legal scholars. When I presented a preliminary version of a paper on duties to some law school colleagues, I got two main responses. The first was that I had misunderstood; if I had a law degree, I would know that duties are ubiquitous since they are everywhere implied. Every right implies a duty—usually a duty of a state but sometimes that of an individual.[43] But a few of these legal colleagues then went on to say, sometimes as an aside, "And besides, it's dangerous to talk of duties." I was confused. How could duties be so commonplace as to be not even worth mentioning and at the same time dangerous? Once again, I realized that responsibilities were a hidden face of rights, always present but sometimes viewed with concern.

By way of explanation, one colleague referred me to a perhaps idiosyncratic case that came before the U.N. Human Rights Committee: *Wackenheim v. France*.[44] This case, also known as the dwarf-tossing case, has taken on an importance beyond its narrow confines. It is seen as creating a precedent that allows states to deny individual rights in the name of an individual responsibility to protect one's own dignity. Dwarf tossing, invented in the 1980s in Australia, is a game in which contestants try to see who can throw a (willing and protected) dwarf the farthest. New York City outlawed dwarf tossing in 1990, as did France. France's prohibition led Mr. Wackenheim, a French citizen and a dwarf, to sue on the grounds that the law "infringed on his autonomy and his right to pursue employment in a difficult job market."[45] The Human Rights Committee upheld the French law, finding that it was contrary to Mr. Wackenheim's dignity to sell himself into dwarf tossing. People are worried about what this case could foreshadow, especially as regards sex work. If a dwarf cannot sell himself into tossing, it is not long, some may reason, before people will be forbidden to sell themselves into sex work because they would be violating their responsibility for their own personal dignity.

Why are duties perceived as simultaneously ubiquitous and dangerous? Why do human rights activists live lives of responsibility but not like to talk about the responsibilities of others? Why would responsibilities be treated as if they were the hidden and shameful face of human rights? My approach to human rights and responsibilities attempts to move us beyond the idea that any defense of responsibilities is an attack on rights.

In this book I divide responsibilities into three domains. The first involves those that are inescapably international. Climate change, for example, is a global problem that must be addressed by global action, but the obligation to participate in this global action falls not only on states, corporations, and international organizations, but also on many other non-state actors and individuals. Privacy and disinformation in the digital age are global issues that require the participation of a diverse set of actors. Because digital problems are related to global corporations such as Facebook and Google, no country can handle the issue alone. The transnational nature of these issues was illustrated when the European Union created a more expansive regulatory regime designed to protect privacy and its actions spilled over into the accounts of Internet users around the world. I explore these global rights in the first part of this book.

The second domain involves rights and duties at the national level, especially the responsibility to vote. Federal, state, and local governments have duties to protect and facilitate the right to vote, but their efforts must be complemented by the actions of citizens who actively exercise their right and responsibility to vote and their responsibilities to encourage others to vote. Unless citizens exercise their duty to vote, the right to vote cannot be fully realized. The second part of the book will look at the responsibility to vote, highlighting U.S. elections and student voting in particular.

The third domain looks at rights and responsibilities on campus around issues of free speech and sexual assault. These issues also involve decentralized compliance decisions in which universities, groups, and individuals within universities have key roles to play in forging the appropriate norms and practices. The book's final chapter will emphasize that this rights-and-responsibilities approach is a framework within which we may ask questions, think and talk about human rights, and strategize for change.[46] It is not a recipe or an action list. Once we have specified the rights that are relevant to a given issue, a rights-and-responsibilities framework requires us to identify all the relevant agents of justice socially connected to the issue and strategize how they could work together more effectively to implement those rights. States will always be crucial actors in this model but never the only ones. The framework may be particularly useful, in fact, when states are unwilling or unable to carry out their responsibilities and other actors must step in. The goal of the book is to move diverse non-state responsibilities from the hidden face of human rights and make them an explicit, necessary, and welcome part of the human rights debates and action.

CHAPTER TWO

Laying Out the Theoretical Groundwork

I came upon the topic of human rights and individual duties or responsibilities while researching my recent book, *Evidence for Hope*, and discovered that the issue was much more important and controversial than I initially understood.[1] *Evidence for Hope* was a full-throated defense of human rights legitimacy and effectiveness against a series of critiques that I believed were unsubstantiated historically and empirically. In this book, I elaborate my own critique or, more correctly, my own recommendations for an improvement in the implementation of human rights via reclaiming responsibility within the framework of robust rights protections.

Individual rights were accompanied by individual duties in the first intergovernmental declaration of human rights: the American Declaration of the Rights and Duties of Man of April 1948. This declaration includes twenty-eight articles on rights and ten articles on individual duties. The duties, each of which receives a full article, are to society, toward children and parents, to receive instruction, to vote, to obey the law, to serve the community and the nation, to contribute to social security and welfare, to pay taxes, to work, and to refrain from political activities in a foreign country. The first item, the duty of the individual "to conduct himself in relation to others that each and every one may fully form and develop his personality," can be read as a responsibility to respect the rights of others. The historical context also supports a more ambitious claim: an individual responsibility to ensure the full development of others' potential.[2]

The duties in the American Declaration were derived from Latin American traditions of Catholic social doctrine, socialist thought, and civic republicanism. In civic-republican tradition, common in both the United States and Latin America in the colonial and postcolonial period, the fulfillment of citizen duties, seen as virtue, was essential to maintaining equality and liberty. This fulfillment required a more active role of the citizen than conventional liberal conceptions.[3] The Mexican delegate who drafted the declaration's duties section also drew ideas about duties from the 1917 Mexican constitution.[4]

The American Declaration in turn had an important influence on the Universal Declaration of Human Rights (UDHR), passed by the U.N. General Assembly eight months later. All of the rights in the UDHR appear first in the American Declaration, but none of the American Declaration's individual duties were incorporated in the final version of the UDHR.[5] The UDHR mentions duties, only in a general way, in Article 29: "Everyone has duties to the community in which alone the free and full development of his personality is possible." The earliest draft of the UDHR, however, mentioned duties many times. The draft of Article 1 even included expansive duties of the individual to the state and to international society or the United Nations: "Everyone owes a duty of loyalty to his State and to the (international society) United Nations. He must accept his just share of responsibility for the performance of such social duties and his share of such common sacrifices as may contribute to the common good."[6] Duties are mentioned eight more times in this draft. These duties, of both states and individuals, were almost entirely removed from the final text.

Onora O'Neill, a philosopher of human rights, noted this absence in her book *Justice across Boundaries*, pointing out that the UDHR, so capacious in its cosmopolitan vision of rights, is almost silent on the agents obligated to carry out these rights. She takes it as a "cavalier" oversight, but the story is more complex.[7] The exclusion of duties was not an oversight but the result of political and philosophical struggles.

When delegates were first drafting the UDHR in 1947, Charles Malik, the Lebanese delegate to the drafting committee, made an impassioned plea to exclude duties. He was a Maronite Christian, a Harvard graduate, and, in Glendon's words, an "existentialist philosopher turned master diplomat."[8] On seeing the first draft, Malik found it " 'astounding' that the first articles . . . should state 'Everyone owes a duty of loyalty to his State.' " He questioned whether an individual owed this loyalty regardless of the state's characteristics, suggesting that an authoritarian state, for example, was not entitled to either duty or loyalty. Malik argued that it "was precisely because the balance had been tipped against the individual and in favor of society that human rights had been violated."[9] Too much emphasis on duties to the state was likely to exacerbate human rights violations rather than ameliorate them.

Malik was not alone in his thinking. He was supported by the governments of the United Kingdom and the United States, which were not sympathetic to the notion of duties.[10] Instead of promoting duties to others, the U.S. delegate to the drafting committee argued, "In the exercise of his rights, everyone is limited by the rights of others."[11] As opposed to the *rights and duties* tradition in Latin America, here we see a *rights vs. rights* tradition characteristic of Anglo-American thought, where individual rights are limited only by the rights of others and are not explicitly socially connected via an individual duty. Glendon has argued that in America rights "tend to be presented as absolute, individual, and independent of any necessary relation to responsibilities."[12] Another possible explanation for why the American and British representatives opposed recognizing duties in the UDHR is that they were suspicious of the role that Catholic social doctrine played as one of the sources of the duties.[13] In the final version of the UDHR, the obligations of states and of other actors were everywhere implied but nowhere spelled out. The declaration begins with a preamble that addresses diverse actors—all peoples and all nations, every individual and every organ of society, as well as member states—and implies but never states the responsibilities of these diverse actors to strive for the universal observance of rights.

With duties largely excluded from the UDHR, the idea that rights are accompanied by an explicit and robust set of individual duties all but disappeared from international human rights law. Neither the International Covenant on Civil and Political Rights nor the International Covenant on Economic, Social, and Cultural Rights, drafted in the 1950s and early 1960s, contains any reference to specific individual duties in the body of the covenants, although they share a statement on duties in their preambles, "realizing that the individual, having duties to other individuals and to the community to which he belongs, is under a responsibility to strive for the promotion and observance of the rights recognized in the present Covenant."

Only one international human rights treaty included more than a sentence in its preamble briefly mentioning duties or responsibilities: the African Charter on Human and Peoples' Rights, also known as the Banjul Charter, drafted in 1979–81. African leaders and jurists wanted a human rights treaty that reflected the historical traditions and values of Africa; foremost among these was the idea of duties and the role of individuals in the community and the family. The focus on the duties of individuals, in three articles and eleven paragraphs, is one of the most innovative features of the Banjul Charter.[14] But the duties of individuals listed in the charter are quite general, and it is not at all clear that they could be enforced legally. Rather, we might see them as serving a more "didactic" function, aimed at stimulating solidarity. In the best sense, these duties were intended to reinforce rights, not give a tool to governments to take away rights.[15]

The preamble of the Banjul Charter recognizes "that the enjoyment of rights and freedoms also implies the performance of duties on the part of everyone," and the body of the charter has an entire chapter on duties. Article 27:1 reads: "Every individual shall have duties towards his family and society, the State and other legally recognized communities and the international community."[16] It is ironic that a region often seen as parochially communitarian reveals a more cosmopolitan understanding of responsibility than any other region of the world. Yet little attention has been paid to the way the Banjul Charter addresses duties or to the fact that it is the only human rights treaty to do so with any specificity.[17] The general neglect of individual responsibility in relation to human rights may be the result of what social scientists call "path-dependent" development. Once the UDHR omitted duties, later human rights treaties—and the ways in which we think and talk about rights—followed suit.

Initiatives to codify responsibilities regained some momentum after the Cold War. At least eight different efforts to draft declarations or resolutions about duties and responsibilities took place between 1993 and 2011.[18] Most of these efforts did not attract widespread attention. Of these, perhaps the most important was in 1997, when, on the eve of the fiftieth anniversary of the UDHR, an organization of world leaders called the InterAction Council proposed a new international agreement: a universal declaration of human responsibilities.[19] Designed to both commemorate and complement the UDHR, the document called for a shared "global ethic" that would balance the rights of individuals with basic human responsibilities. While many of the document's signers came from Europe and North America, they were by no means a homogeneous clique. Some members, such as Jimmy Carter and Oscar Arias Sánchez (the former president of Costa Rica), were Nobel Peace Prize winners committed to human rights. Others, like Helmut Schmidt (the chair of the group) and Valéry

Giscard d'Estaing, had stood at the helm of traditional European powers. The list also included leaders from smaller states, such as Lee Kuan Yew, the former premier of Singapore who famously prioritized efficient governance, economic growth, and a concern for "Asian values" above universal human rights.[20] Even Henry Kissinger and Robert McNamara, two of the Cold War's most prominent realists, signed on as supporters of the initiative, along with an array of other leaders representing academia, international organizations, and NGOs.

Despite their diverse backgrounds and ideologies, the backers of the declaration agreed on an unambiguous and ambitious premise: "[All] people, to the best of their knowledge and ability, have a responsibility to foster a better social order, both at home and globally."[21] Noting that an overemphasis on rights could lead to "conflict, division and endless dispute," the draft declaration called for all people to acknowledge the fact of responsibilities and then outlined specific obligations.[22]

The proposed Declaration of Human Responsibilities failed to gain widespread support. Rather than complementing the UDHR, as envisioned, it drew a barrage of criticism from almost every sector. Legal scholars argued that individuals already possessed obligations that were firmly established in international law, making the declaration superfluous and vague.[23] Feminist scholars saw patriarchal motivations behind the call to balance rights and responsibilities, particularly in the document's insistence on addressing family and domestic responsibilities.[24] Amnesty International alleged that if passed, the declaration would "muddy" the understanding of universal human rights and might help justify authoritarian regimes in denying their citizens basic rights.[25]

The former executive director of Amnesty International USA, William Schulz, explained Amnesty's thinking by stressing two different ways in which the word *responsibility* can be used with regard to human rights. One involves responsibility in terms of implementation: "If we wish to have rights, we need to be responsible for implementing them by doing A, B, or C. I can't imagine too many human advocates who would disagree with that. But governments and other human rights evaders usually use *responsibility* in a second sense as a check on freedom."[26]

Amnesty's objection to the Declaration of Human Responsibilities had to do with the second meaning. For example, the report explaining the declaration stated, "If we have a right to partake in our country's political process and elect our leaders, then we have the obligation to participate and ensure that the best leaders are chosen." Schulz clarified that no one had any problem with the first part of the sentence because it involved using responsibility to implement a freedom, but "the second part of the sentence implied a limit to our 'right to partake in our country's political process' by saying that we would be acting 'irresponsibly' if we failed to pick the best leaders. This second meaning of *responsibility* is the one resorted to all the time by tyrants and human rights violators—[who say], 'We have a responsibility to respect our leaders, our country's security, our traditional values, etc., and rights ought not supersede those greater responsibilities."[27] This distinction of two meanings of *responsibility* is relevant for this book, as my emphasis will be consistently on the first meaning of responsibilities as tools to more fully implement rights.

In response to calls for greater emphasis on obligations, the U.N. General Assembly passed the Declaration on the Right and Responsibility of Individuals, Groups, and Organs of Society to Promote and Protect Universally Recognized Human Rights and Fundamental Freedoms.[28] Despite its title, however, this document does not stress individual responsibility in human rights law. Instead, it mentions responsibility only in passing and reinforces the traditional view that the duty to respect or promote human rights lies mainly with states.[29] Clearly, the "human responsibilities movement" proved less of a threat to the traditional human rights regime than scholars and activists feared at the time.

DEFINING KEY CONCEPTS

In this book, I use the term *human rights* broadly to include the political, civil, economic, and social rights in the UDHR and human rights law, as well as demands for new rights, such as the right to a clean environment or to digital privacy. In this sense, I adopt what Charles Beitz calls "a practical conception of human rights," in that I use the "doctrine and practice of human rights as we find them in international political life" as my starting point for defining human rights.[30] I prefer to use existing international human rights law as my starting point (instead of the ideas about rights from a single country or philosopher) because it represents an "overlapping international political consensus."[31] There are still lots of disagreements about human rights in the world, but there is also considerable consensus and support. Starting with existing international norms drafted through exhaustive debate and consultation among many states has the virtue of being less ethnocentric than having the analyst substitute her own normative criteria. Examined closely, the process of drafting and implementing human rights law provides a model for deliberative, nonviolent, and noncoercive processes of global governance and change.

I refer to rights and responsibilities using the terms *norms* and *practices*. Norms are standards of appropriate behavior. They tell us what is expected, what is right, and what is wrong.[32] In the case of international human rights, most norms are embedded in "hard law"—that is, in treaties that have been ratified by many states and are thus legally binding for those states. But some human rights norms are part of only "soft law," or they appear in various declarations and resolutions that are not treaties. Many of the new rights I discuss, such as the right to a clean environment or the right to digital privacy, are not yet incorporated into human rights treaties, but we can still think of them as norms.

Practices, on the other hand, are "performances" and "socially meaningful patterns of actions" that express preferences and beliefs.[33] Like practicing the piano, they are repeated and patterned, and this repetition is what gives them meaning and structures interaction.[34] Much of the work of the human rights movement involves well-known practices, both legal and non-legal, such as one's writing letters to governments to protest human rights violations, writing reports, litigating in domestic and international courts, and making statements in various U.N. human rights bodies.

In addition to established norms and law, as well as well-developed and explicit practices, the human rights advocacy community also, I argue, has robust practices of responsibility. But it does not yet have explicit norms about the responsibility of non-state actors in implementing human rights.

Rights are often divided in multiple ways: civil and political versus economic and social rights or negative versus positive rights (those that call on the government to refrain from doing something, such as torture or censorship, versus those that require it to take some positive action, such as building a school). There is also a division between rights violations that take place in the public sphere (such as police abuse) and those that take place in the private sphere (such as female genital cutting).

The most important distinction I will use in this book, however, is not common in the literature: the distinction I introduced in chapter 1 between rights with decentralized compliance decisions and those with centralized compliance decisions.[35] Virtually all private-sphere rights violations involve decentralized compliance decisions, but some public-sphere rights violations are also decentralized. For instance, while the right to be free from torture and the right to be free from the death penalty are both classic "negative rights," the death penalty is highly centralized and torture is more decentralized in that it can occur in many police stations or military barracks. I argue that networked responsibilities are particularly important to implement rights with very decentralized compliance.

Scholars disagree, especially across disciplines, about the precise meanings of *duty*, *responsibility*, and *obligation*. The term *duty* comes from old French, where it meant something due or owed a feudal lord by a vassal or a serf, and it has not completely shaken off this connection to status differentials and coercion.[36] *Duty* is also associated with religion, as we saw in the influence of Catholic social doctrine on the American Declaration of the Rights and Duties of Man. Some consensus has also emerged that *duty* is more legal and precise than *responsibility*.[37] *Obligation* is also more associated with states. One author has even claimed that *obligation* is a term "reserved for the duties of the state," not individuals or institutions.[38]

Elizabeth Jelin is the clearest about the reasons for her choice for the concept to use: "Duty and obligation bear a coercive imperative: but responsibilities . . . are broader and extend beyond duty . . . [including] a civic commitment centered on active participation in public life (the responsibilities of citizenship) as well as symbolic and ethical aspects that confer a sense of belonging, a sense of community."[39] For these reasons, I believe that neither *duty* nor *obligation* is a persuasive term to use to promote collective action against injustice.

Responsibility, on the other hand, is a relatively "new virtue," or at least a newly named one. It was mentioned for the first time in the late eighteenth century, including notably in the *Federalist Papers*.[40] Figure 1, tracking the prevalence of the words "rights," "duties," and "responsibilities," in *New York Times* articles from 1855 to 2017, supports the idea that both rights and duties are the older terms and that responsibilities is a newer concept. My research assistants and I found similar results when looking for the prevalence of the terms duties, rights, and responsibilities in a Google Books Ngram Viewer and in U.S. political party platform language from 1900 to 2018.[41] Each of these sources supports the argument that discussions of duties and rights were equally prominent in the

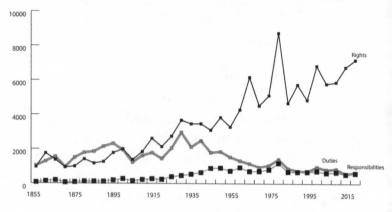

Figure 1: Mentions of "rights," "duties," and "responsibilities"
in *New York Times* articles, 1855–2017.

nineteenth and early twentieth centuries, while discussions of
responsibilities were absent. Somewhere in the mid-twentieth
century, around the time duties were left out of the UDHR,
rights became the far more prevalent concept compared to
duties, reinforcing the idea that since that time we have lived
in an "Age of Rights," where discussions of duties and responsibilities have been far less common. Since the second half of
the twentieth century, references to responsibilities have become somewhat more prevalent but not enough to begin
speaking of a new "Age of Responsibilities," as some authors
do.[42] These sources all refer to English-language sources, and
it is quite possible that patterns would look different if we
looked at sources in Spanish or French, for example.

The term responsibility has taken center stage in my field
of international relations to denote a variety of international
issues such as corporate social responsibility,[43] sovereignty-as-
responsibility,[44] and the idea of common but differentiated

38

responsibility in environmental policy.[45] Nowhere has attention to responsibilities been more prominent than in relation to human rights, as, for example, the Responsibility to Protect (R2P) and businesses' responsibilities to respect human rights.[46] For this reason, responsibility appears to be the term with more resonance in the international arena.

There is no agreed-upon definition of responsibility. I will rely on a distinction, highlighted by some philosophers, between backward-looking and forward-looking forms of responsibility.[47] Backward-looking responsibility involves blame and often legal liability leading to sanctions. This is what Iris Young calls the "liability model" of responsibility.[48] Young recognizes that responsibility is generally understood to concern who caused harm and how that party should be held accountable. In the liability model, accountability often involves litigation—demanding that people, states, or corporations pay remedies or damages or send individuals to prison. In this model, attention to responsibility implies legal duties, something many did not want to write into human rights law. In general, lawyers and legal theorists discuss responsibility by thinking about how to determine liability, and even when lawyers turn to more political discussions of responsibility, they focus on questions like "Under what condition is it appropriate to praise or blame agents for their actions (or their omissions)?"[49] Given that many human rights activists and academics are lawyers, it is not surprising that the liability model is the most common model of responsibility in the human rights world.

Like Young, I do not reject the liability model; rather, I think that it is appropriate in some human rights contexts but not others. I believe firmly, for example, in individual legal accountability for mass atrocity. In my book *The Justice Cascade*, I documented the trend toward increasing legal liability for mass atrocity and showed that trying government officials for human rights violations can contribute to improvements in core human rights.[50] Nevertheless, individual criminal accountability is only one small part of the solution, and for most human rights issues we also need to focus on forward-looking responsibilities.

In this book, I am primarily interested in forward-looking political responsibilities. I will also use responsibility in the first sense mentioned by William Schulz, primarily as a means of implementing rights and not of restricting them. This does not mean that backward-looking responsibilities are unnecessary, but they cannot address many of the complex, decentralized issues that characterize human rights today. With regard to climate change, for example, it is no longer sufficient to focus on who is to blame for global warming. Instead, we need to think about how everyone connected to the problem can work together to try to limit emissions.

Responsibility carries with it so much baggage in current political debates in the United States over welfare policy, however, that some of my colleagues have argued that it is too tainted a term to use for my purposes.[51] Some believe the term responsibility is too associated with an ideology of radical individualism that places the blame on welfare recipients for their own misfortune.

But responsibility is too powerful a term to cede when it has been long associated elsewhere with notions of care for others and community, as in the Banjul Charter. I will occa-

sionally switch to use the terms duties or obligations, not in-
terchangeably, but when the literature and the history I discuss use those terms.

The philosophers whose works I have found most useful in
thinking about responsibilities, such as Hannah Arendt, Iris
Marion Young, Max Weber, and Onora O'Neill, do not make
us choose between rights and responsibilities. Instead they
oblige us constantly to hold both in our minds and actions.

Weber, in his essay "Politics as a Vocation," used the phrase
"ethic of responsibility" to denote one of the most important
qualities for people acting in politics. For Weber, this ethic did
not mean just taking responsibility but also being morally "an-
swerable for the (foreseeable) consequences of one's actions"
or inactions. He stressed the difference between an ethic of
responsibility and an ethic of intention. An ethic of intention
referred to people who want only to see that the flame of protest against injustice is not extinguished.[52] Weber advocated
instead a combination of passion, sense of responsibility, and
judgment. Passion—belief in some real cause—must always be
there, but it must be disciplined by responsibility and judgment.[53] He also advocated a form of responsibility that looked
to the future, not to the past. He criticized the search for
"guilty men" and instead argued that the "true concerns of the
politician [are] the future and his responsibility towards it."[54]

Following Weber, I advocate an ethic of responsibility
rather than one of pure intentions regardless of consequences. Weber takes consequences seriously, but he was not a

consequentialist in the sense of thinking that consequences are the only relevant factor in deciding whether an action is morally right. In this sense, his approach for making moral decisions differs from that of modern consequentialists like Peter Singer in that such an approach looks at both intentions and consequences.[55] Weber understood that people acting in politics should continue to be motivated by their passions and intentions but that they also need to think about consequences. Joseph Nye offers a contemporary version of such an approach with his "three-dimensional ethics" framework, which takes intentions, means, and consequences into account simultaneously.[56] What I understand as taking consequences seriously may be different from what Weber intended, but I share his belief that the findings of science can guide us in thinking about consequences.[57] Modern scientific and social science research has much to say about the probable impact of different actions. Throughout this book I will advocate forward-looking networked forms of responsibility for which there is some evidence of significant effectiveness. For example, with regard to individual responsibility for climate change, I will argue that individuals and organizations should work to reduce long-distance air travel because this is one of the most effective ways of reducing the lifestyle-related creation of greenhouse gases, second only to going completely car-free.[58]

Hannah Arendt's understanding of political responsibility, and especially her book *Eichmann in Jerusalem*, also influences the discussion here. The parts of the book that are most relevant have to do with responsibility not in the sense of guilt, but in the positive sense of an expression of citizenship. Arendt's discussion of how the Danish people and government took political responsibility for protecting Jews in Denmark during World War II from repression and deportation to the death camps is such a case. The Danish government refused the Nazi demand to use the yellow star to distinguish between Jews and non-Jews. Later, when the Germans began deportations, the Danish government warned the Jewish community, and Danish citizens arranged for most of the Jews in Denmark to be transported to neutral Sweden in a small flotilla of fishing boats. Arendt argues that the case of Danish rescuers should be "required reading for every political science student." Even as Arendt dissected the great power of the totalitarian state, she never ignored issues of political responsibility.[59] Even so, there was a vast critical literature in response to *Eichmann in Jerusalem* because some readers thought that a key concept in the book—"the banality of evil"—served to trivialize or downplay Eichmann's responsibility for his actions.[60] But for Arendt, political responsibility was a high calling; for example, she referred to the Danish rescue as "the result of an authentically political sense, an inbred comprehension of the requirements and responsibilities of citizenship."[61] It was very different from guilt.[62] It was because Eichmann was thoughtless and incapable of distinguishing right from wrong that he was incapable of these responsibilities of citizenship.

Arendt believed that political responsibility derives from common membership in a country.[63] But citizenship in a country is too constrained a criterion for the kind of international political responsibility I discuss here. Mathias Risse conceives of human rights as membership rights in a world society and then spells out the global responsibilities implied for different actors, especially states.[64] In *Responsibility for Justice*, Iris Young argues that it is the condition of "social connection" to a structural injustice, rather than citizenship, that yields responsibility.[65] Following Young, I speak of political responsibility that derives from social connection rather than citizenship.

Finally, Onora O'Neill provides one of the most explicit analyses of responsibility and international human rights, arguing that rights can "be realized only if the counterpart obligations were held by competent agents." She maintains that there are multiple agents of justice who carry moral obligations to further rights, including, to an important extent, the victims of human rights violations. States are of course always the primary bearers of obligations to respect and fulfill rights, but excessive focus on states ignores the reality that many are unwilling to respect rights and/or unable to enforce them. O'Neill rightly criticizes discussions of human rights that "are silent or vague about the agents of justice, or about their specific duties, and assume without argument that the relevant duties all fall on states." Human rights declarations and treaties, she notes, reflect the assumption that the state is the primary agent of accountability and virtually never discuss other actors as bearers of obligations.[66]

O'Neill argues that an emphasis on obligation would help human rights victims sustain themselves as agents. "We must be committed," she writes, "to strategies and policies that enable them to become and to remain agents. If we do anything less, we do not view others as doers like ourselves."[67] Yascha Mounk, in a similar vein, writes that people's "equal status as full citizens [is] fatally undermined if there are some citizens who are considered to be fully responsible agents and others who are not."[68] Some victims of torture and rape understand that the label "victim" may deny them agency and thus prefer to be called "torture survivors" or "rape survivors."

For Young, a key feature of forward-looking responsibility is that it can be discharged only through collective action with others. I agree, but I do not exclude individual actions taken within the context of collective action. There is often a productive interaction between individual and collective action, and forward-looking responsibility may be discharged through a combination of both. For example, voting, a civic responsibility, is ultimately an individual act, though it is usually embedded in collective action.

One of the theorists who influenced Young, Henry Richardson, argued for a moral "specialized division of deliberative responsibility" for institutions and individuals engaged in forward-looking responsibility. In his view, we are responsible for a range of concerns, but since our responsibilities are not always clearly spelled out, there is room for agents to deliberate.[69] Young, following in this line of thought, saw forward-looking responsibility as more open and discretionary than duty: "It is up to the agents who have a responsibility to decide what to do to discharge it within the limits of other moral considerations."[70] Mark Blitz agrees with this idea: he sees responsibility as a virtue that is consistent with the modern liberal understanding of self, in which attachments are always voluntary.[71]

Because forward-looking responsibility is discretionary, Young says that there is no single set of rules or methods for deciding what to do. But she provides four parameters that agents can use for reasoning about their actions and those of others: power, privilege, interest, and collective ability. These derive largely from the social positions each actor occupies. Young illustrates what she means by these parameters using examples from global campaigns against sweatshops. *Power* refers to the capacity actors have to influence structural processes. *Privilege* often follows from power, but there can be groups or people with relatively little power who have a privileged position with regard to some injustice issues. Young gives the example of the privilege that middle-class clothing consumers have in relation to sweatshops in the developing world because they are able to change their consumption habits without serious deprivation. Young also argues that *interests* do not always need to be seen as contrary to responsibility for justice because sometimes agents' interests coincide with their responsibilities. I will argue below, for example, that college women have a strong interest in taking forward-looking responsibility around issues of sexual assault on campus. Finally, some agents have more *collective ability* because, for example, they can "draw on the resources of already organized entities and use them in new ways for trying to promote change." On her issue of sweatshops, Young points to unions, church groups, stockholder organizations, and student groups with leverage on the purchasing decisions of college bookstores as examples of agents with collective ability.[72]

This book embraces this idea of the open and discretionary ways in which agents may discharge forward-looking responsibilities. As such, I will not propose or outline any list of recommended responsibilities. But I am very aware of Young's four parameters, and it is no accident that the book is mainly addressed to people with privilege and collective ability to exercise responsibility. People reading this book may not think of themselves as privileged or having collective ability to assume and exercise responsibility, but I will argue that we need to realistically assess our privilege and capacity to motivate action. Many people I address here have privilege in the sense that they themselves can make choices or they work within institutions that can make consequential choices with regard to exercising responsibility.

Since I embrace the idea that agents have discretion in how they discharge forward-looking responsibilities, I will not offer any single list of policies, for example, by which institutions or individuals discharge their responsibility on climate change. Some institutions may choose to install more energy-efficient lighting, add solar panels, or recycle and compost. Individuals can do the same and also walk or bike to work each day, taking fewer plane trips, or choose not to eat meat. Such actions may seem ineffective or uncoordinated. But Richardson argues that such a moral division of labor is "a vehicle for constituting and coordinating complex cooperative action, which has no simple overall purpose. This system lacks an all-knowing and wholly wise administrator."[73] He does not address international institutions, the environment, or human rights at all, and yet his formulation is useful in thinking about international responsibilities.

Reducing climate change or promoting global human rights, for example, requires constituting and coordinating complex cooperative action, and the international system indeed lacks an all-knowing administrator. We do not have a single climate change treaty or organization but instead what

Robert Keohane and David G. Victor call a regime complex: a loosely coupled set of narrowly focused regulatory institutions and norms that help coordinate the mainly voluntary commitments of each state.[74] Within states, climate policy also involves complex cooperative action. Governments could assign each individual or institution specific duties to help states meet their emission goals, but it may be more effective to build norms and practices of responsibility in the hope that individuals and institutions will use their best judgment in deciding how to control emissions.

Such a discretionary system of promoting responsibility is imperfect but better than existing alternatives. The Chinese government is planning a "social credit system" for what it calls a national reputation system.[75] Data will be gathered on individual citizens to see if they are doing their duty to conform to societal integrity, a kind of responsibility defined by the Chinese state. Citizens with low scores may be blocked from purchasing domestic flights, sending their children to certain schools, or even getting some jobs. This is a responsibility system, but a draconian one, where rights and responsibilities are not balanced: responsibility trumps rights. It is the threat of such policies that makes it important not to write extensive lists of legal duties into law and instead to stress the exercise of responsibilities through voluntary collective action.

Richardson's notion of a "specialized division of deliberative responsibility" and Young's idea of openness and discretion together give us a workable definition of how responsibilities might function in the realm of human rights and the environment. There are effective ways of coordinating the promotion of rights and multiple exercises of responsibility, which often involve legal, ethical, and political deliberation and struggle. Our responsibilities as individuals, and the responsibilities of multiple institutions of which we may be a part, are to take up some modest share of this complex cooperative action.

Roxane Gay, writing in the *New York Times* "Sunday Review" in the guise of an advice columnist, expresses the same idea in a way that is both lighthearted and direct. Her imagined advice seeker asks, "Am I terrible for not doing more?" and signs herself "Apathetic idealist." Roxanne answers, "It is difficult to balance activism and investing in the greater good with demands of an ordinary life. It's hard to know what to pay attention to and what to respond to and how. . . . The grand thing about collective effort is that we can generally trust that someone is out in the world doing social justice work when we are too tired or burned out to join in. . . . I've also been trying to pick one issue at a time. . . . If I focus on just one issue and apply genuine effort and attention to it, I just might contribute something useful."[76] She feels responsible for doing her part for social justice but recognizes that others are also doing their share.

Sometimes our modest share is extremely pressing and demanding. Rescuers during the Holocaust or in the genocide in Rwanda, for instance, faced agonizing choices about whether or not to help endangered others and how much risk to take or impose on their families. Our training in rights and responsibilities should at least prepare us for the unlikely circumstance that we might be asked to take very major responsibilities for the lives of others.

More often, the link between our modest actions and any change in the world may seem distant and even far-fetched.

Did that letter I wrote, the petition I signed, the march I joined, or the voting campaign we are trying to organize make any difference at all? Our individual and collective actions accumulate in unexpected ways, at times marvelous, more often obscure, mysterious, exhausting, and frustrating. As Richardson points out, the whole system of divided moral responsibility is also dynamic. "It changes in response to new aspirations and problems."[77] This too fits well with the human rights regime. Human rights involve many issues, and different ones come to the fore at different times, as when the issues of sexual violence and harassment exploded with the #MeToo movement in Trump's America.

People often say they want more precision: what exactly are our responsibilities? The nature of the human rights system and the nature of responsibilities mean that there are no precise or definitive answers. We know that for every right, there are duty bearers responsible for helping ensure the enjoyment of that right and that most often the primary duty bearer is the state. But we also know, historically, that continuing to create more legal rights without sufficient attention to implementing our existing rights has led to disillusionment and pessimism. We need to pay more political and ethical attention to the work of multiple agents of justice. We need more actors to use the openness and discretion of forward-looking responsibility not to evade it, but to choose it. We need to understand that the complex global action that is international human rights requires some division of labor. Human rights advocates, working in transnational advocacy networks, have been doing this for decades, and in some cases (such as anti-slavery and women's suffrage), for centuries.[78]

I believe Charles Malik was right. In 1947, when an international agreement on human rights was being drafted for the first time, it did not make sense to preface those rights with caveats about individual duties, especially duties to states. Now, however, seventy years have passed; it is time to reopen the debate on responsibilities and their relation to rights. Declarations about the protection of rights are now part of a large complex of international human rights law and institutions to enforce it. Human rights is one of the dominant moral discourses of our age.[79] The balance of which Malik spoke has been tipped, at least rhetorically, in favor of rights over responsibilities. It now makes sense to balance the equation with a political and ethical discussion of the importance of responsibilities in fulfilling rights. But *balance* is not even the right word here. Responsibilities are simply necessary for making the enjoyment of rights possible in the first place, logically, politically, and practically.

Malik was also correct when he said that governments and courts could manipulate arguments about duty. For example, in 2014 the Ugandan Court of Appeals, sitting as the constitutional court, used the duty language in the Banjul Charter to defend the criminalization of homosexual sex. The court cited the provision of the charter that says individuals have the duty to "preserve and strengthen positive African cultural values" and "to contribute to the moral well-being of society." It neglected to cite the section that said this should be done "in the spirit of tolerance."[80] As we think about a rights-and-responsibilities framework, we must also be aware of the ability of self-interested governments to manipulate ideas about responsibility.

My purpose is not to propose another declaration of human responsibilities or to place a special burden on individuals. It is, rather, to insist that for the enjoyment and implementation of rights, other agents, including individuals, must take some responsibilities for the fulfillment of rights. Examples of networked responsibility are everywhere, but somehow, in the "Age of Rights," open discussion of non-state responsibilities has fallen to the wayside. We need to recover it.

CHAPTER THREE

Global Rights and Responsibilities: Climate Change and Digital Defense against the Dark Arts

How are global rights and responsibilities connected in practice? What does a "social connection model" of forward-looking responsibility look like? Does Young's argument that responsibility can be "discretionary" mean that individuals and groups can simply choose what to do—for example, with regard to climate change? How can we apply Weber's notion of an ethic of responsibility to reality?

FORWARD-LOOKING RESPONSIBILITY FOR CLIMATE CHANGE

Many environmental activists have begun to address environmental problems in terms of rights—new concepts of rights as belonging to trees, rivers, and even Mother Earth, as well as the more conventional rights of individuals to clean water and a safe environment. To be effective, rights-based approaches must also stress the responsibilities of a broad range of agents of justice.

Historically, the main responsibility for environmental degradation has followed the "polluter pays principle": the party producing pollution is liable for the resulting damage to the environment. This is a clear example of backward-looking responsibility. The polluter pays principle is an essential aspect of environmental law and has been useful in many cases, but it is hopelessly insufficient against climate change. The responsible parties are too numerous, most cannot be identified or are long gone, and those that still exist do not have the capacity, by themselves, to solve the problem. Backward-looking responsibilities must be combined with forward-looking responsibilities, including the responsibilities of actors who are not directly to blame.

The most promising rights-based approaches to climate change focus on the rights of future generations; these already involve forward-looking responsibility. For example, a human rights and social justice organization in Colombia called Dejusticia filed a climate change and deforestation lawsuit on behalf of twenty-five child plaintiffs. This was the first environmental case in Latin America that focused on the rights of the young. The plaintiffs argued that their rights to life, health, water, food, and a healthy environment were threatened by the dramatic increase in deforestation in the Colombian Amazon.[1] In 2018, the Supreme Court of Justice of Colombia ruled in the plaintiffs' favor, a result one expert called "one of the strongest environmental decisions ever issued by any court in the world."[2]

Neither Dejusticia's lawsuit nor the Supreme Court of Justice's response relied on backward-looking liability. The court ordered the government to present an action plan to combat deforestation and to build an "intergenerational pact for the life of the Colombian Amazon." It identified several agents of justice—including the plaintiffs, their lawyers at Dejusticia, the Colombian government, and research and scientific organizations—as responsible for developing and implementing a plan to protect the Amazon. Deforestation was central because it is the main source of carbon emissions in Colombia and is also central to the government's commitment in the Paris Agreement at the U.N. Climate Change Conference.

The young plaintiffs and their lawyers are already exercising their own responsibility by serving as spokespeople in their communities and working with Dejusticia to craft the content of the intergenerational pact.[3] The agreement must include "national, regional, and local actions of a preventative, obligatory, corrective, and pedagogical nature," and it requires that "all the relevant actors . . . reach commitments to protect the life of the Colombian Amazon" that take into account "common but differentiated responsibilities, as well as respective capacities."[4] This pact exemplifies a social connection model of responsibility.

Climate Ethics and Networked Responsibility

Out of the vast philosophical literature on climate ethics, I will focus here on a recent line of reflection about the connected responsibilities of diverse actors, including individuals, in relation to climate change.[5] Iris Young's idea of forward-looking responsibility and her social connection model of responsibility have found an echo among climate change authors. Simon Caney, for example, agrees about the need for a more forward-looking approach to responsibility that focuses on avoiding harm. He writes, "The burden of combating the problem should be shared fairly among the duty-bearers. An agent's responsibility, then, is to do her fair share."[6] Have we, for example, done everything possible not only to lobby our government to change its policies, but also to limit our own carbon footprint? Some authors believe that if many more of us did this, over a lifetime, personal emissions reductions in themselves could make a substantial contribution to slowing climate change.[7] In addition to their actual impact, these efforts could have "communicative value" that encourages others to follow our example.[8] In this way, our individual emission reductions, which in isolation have little effect on overall emission reductions, may "trigger—more effective and efficient—collective types of action."[9] In this way, individual action can address the collective action problem of free riding. But to do so, we must move beyond our own interests and think about the impacts of our actions on future generations. Our responsibility is thus both to act individually and to make sure this action connects to broader efforts to organize collectively.[10] Finally, this model can be faster than institutional change. "National policies and major energy transformations often take decades to change locked-in infrastructure and institutions, but behavioural shifts have the potential to be more rapid and widespread."[11] Augustin Fragnière, in a survey of the literature on climate change and ethics, concludes that "virtually every author," even authors who deny that individuals have a duty to reduce their personal carbon footprints, "acknowledges that individuals have some duty to promote collective action."[12]

At this time in U.S. history, when the federal government has withdrawn from the Paris Agreement, it is all the more important to stress how diverse actors can carry out their environmental responsibilities. All people connected to the problem of climate change and able to act, even young people who could never be blamed or held liable, have these responsibilities. Here, Iris Young's point that responsibility is conceptually more open and discretionary offers us a flexible approach that encourages action without making actors feel overwhelmed.

To help my students understand how they contribute to climate change both positively and negatively, I have introduced them to carbon footprint exercises.[13] Each of us calculates our own carbon footprint, answering a series of questions about such things as how far we drive each week, how many plane trips we take, and how much we pay for gas and electricity. We log individual actions we have taken to reduce our carbon footprints; for me these include moving to a very small house within walking distance of my office, installing solar panels, turning down the thermostat in the winter, no longer eating beef, composting, recycling, and walking or biking instead of driving. Nevertheless, when I add my domestic and international travel into the calculator, my footprint grows to well above the average. Just one international plane trip erases all my efforts at composting and recycling.

The Harvard Climate Change Task Force reinforced the importance of travel for climate change. When my colleague William Clark delivered the report of the Climate Change Task Force, of which he was the co-chair, to the Harvard Kennedy School faculty, he concluded that changes in the Kennedy School building had gone a long way toward reducing our emissions. We had added insulation, solar panels, LED lighting, composting, and recycling. Now, Clark told us, we needed to address the next frontier: the environmental impact of institutional and individual choices about travel, food, and investment. Yes, he said, telling a group of Harvard faculty to restrict their travel was like telling gun owners to give up their guns. Yet he also knew that the Kennedy School could not continue to reduce carbon emissions unless it addressed institutional and individual choices about travel. Clark gave an example from his own experience as a climate researcher. He was invited to a one-day conference in Singapore on climate change. He told the conference organizers that he thought the impact of his travel on climate change couldn't justify his presence in Singapore for one day but that he would be happy to make his presentation via Skype from Boston. When they pointed out that he would have to present at two o'clock in the morning, he countered that it would be far better to present at such a time than to fly twenty hours for a one-day workshop. This is a good example of how thinking about individual and organizational responsibilities forms one part of a collective solution to climate change.

There is a common belief that individuals can do little to contribute to the fight against climate change. My research and that of other scholars about how social change happens reveal that norm change is often led by individual and institutional norm entrepreneurs, whose actions are essential to pressure for and coalesce changes in norms and practices by a wider range of actors.[14] Most people assume that greenhouse gases primarily come from industrial emissions and that individual choices have little impact. As one blogger wrote, "Dear

Humans, Industry, Not Your Activities, Is Causing Climate Change."[15] But emissions are the result of production and consumption. Consumers, both individual and institutional, make choices about consumption that influence production. To suggest that industry is responsible for emissions but that "human" (consumer) activities are unrelated is naïve. Individuals and institutions can influence emissions by changing what and how much they consume or by insisting, even when they do not reduce ultimate consumption, that they prefer goods and services produced in ways that are better for the environment or people.[16] Most important, however, is that consumers make an impact when they organize collectively to demand change. Communicating their individual consumer choices in order to fuel collective action is as important as the choices themselves.

In late 2017, transportation overtook electricity generation as the top source of greenhouse gases in the United States for the first time since the late 1970s.[17] The responsibilities of diverse actors—including state and local governments, corporations, NGOs, educational institutions, and individuals—to regulate and modify transportation emissions thus cannot be an irrelevant or insignificant consideration. It was exactly this kind of responsibility that Clark was advocating for Harvard University, for the Kennedy School, and for professors and staff. Once again, individual choices do not contradict collective action. My personal choice about taking fewer plane trips is not something I do *instead of* organizing politically but something that complements collective action.

Once we have accepted our responsibilities to take action against climate change, what kinds of actions should we take?

How do we engage in what Weber called an "ethic of responsibility" so that we not only express good intentions, but also take effective actions? We can start by learning what forms of responsibility are likely to be most effective.

A new study by Seth Wynes and Kimberly Nicholas of thirty-nine peer-reviewed papers, government reports, and web-based programs outlined the top ways individuals can reduce their carbon footprints.[18] Based on their research, the authors recommend four high-impact actions: having one child fewer, living car-free, avoiding airplane travel, and eating a plants-based diet. These seem radical, but if you read the article carefully, you find that avoiding just one round-trip transatlantic flight a year is the third most effective way to reduce emissions, after having fewer children and living car-free for a year. Foregoing one round-trip transatlantic (or equivalent) flight each year would cut a person's emissions of carbon dioxide (CO_2) by 1,600 kilograms. Getting rid of your car for a year would cut 2,400 kilograms. In other words, reducing your travel by one-and-a-half transatlantic airplane trips has as much impact as getting rid of your car for a year. These actions have far greater impact than other commonly recommended practices, like comprehensive recycling or changing your light bulbs.[19] But again, we don't have to think in either/or terms. It is not as though I will stop recycling or discard my energy-efficient light bulbs now that I am trying to limit my air travel.

The study's recommendation to have fewer children provoked a critique of the premise that children's carbon emissions get charged to their parents. One author called it a "category error" to compare not having a child to other actions.[20]

For example, can I reduce my own footprint by charging my emissions to my parents? If we eliminate not having a child and instead focus on the actions for which we can all agree we are responsible, not taking a round-trip transatlantic flight is the second most impactful thing we can do, right after not driving a car for a year.

Many people will find these recommendations too demanding and decide it is easier to avoid these hard changes. I too find it very hard to reduce my air travel. I grew up in two small provincial midwestern towns in South Dakota and Minnesota and even as a child dreamed of escape to cosmopolitan international locations. One of my early plans for a job was to be a stewardess. To this day, I find it difficult to imagine that one could do too much international travel. And I'm an international relations scholar; travel for research and conferences is simply a necessary part of my job. I worry that I can't do my job properly if I travel abroad less. So it was useful for me to return to Iris Young's four parameters that agents can use for reasoning about their actions: power, privilege, interest, and collective ability. Like many professionals in the United States, I am privileged and have an ability to act. Objectively, I know that my career will not be harmed by giving up one international trip a year, and indeed, my quality of life may improve! At the Kennedy School, most of my colleagues could also give up one round-trip transatlantic or equivalent trip each year without significant harm to their academic careers or personal lives.

William Clark and his Climate Change Task Force have launched a pilot project to start trying to measure how we would implement voluntary faculty commitment to give up some international travel and replace it with a video presentation. As important, we need to work with the many Kennedy School staff directing programming to designate one event where staff members follow Clark's example and Skype in an international expert rather than fly him or her to Boston. The same Wynes and Nicholas study also reaffirmed Clark's point about food choices, showing a plant-based diet to be the third most effective lifestyle choice for combatting climate change. This point was reinforced by the findings of Gidon Eshel, a geophysicist who studies the climate impact of food choices. Although Eshel himself advocates and practices a purely plant-based diet, he recognizes that this is not for everyone and also recommends alternatives. For instance, he told an interviewer for the *Harvard Magazine* that if people wanted to make one food choice likely to have the most impact on climate change, they should give up beef and substitute poultry.[21] Eshel is a genuine norm entrepreneur, moving beyond his scientific work to take his message to the general public in such popular documentaries as *Planeat* and Leonardo DiCaprio's *Before the Flood*. He believes that individual dietary choices can play a key role in climate change policy: they "get to tip the scale of environmental, social, and political contests." For Eshel, eating healthy foods that use less land "is one of the callings of our time."[22]

When we are talking about the impact of individual action on climate change, the forward-looking responsibilities of some people matter much more than others. As Young pointed out, power and privilege matter. Individuals with reasonable alternatives, capacity, or resources should be seen as having more forward-looking responsibility because "a) they

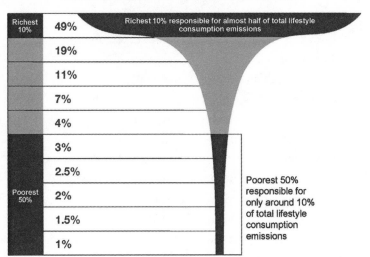

Figure 2: Global income deciles and associated lifestyle consumption emissions.

The material—figure 1 on page 4, from "Oxfam Media Briefing–02/12/2015"—is adapted by the author with the permission of Oxfam, Oxfam House, John Smith Drive, Cowley, Oxford OX4 2JY UK, www.oxfam.org.uk. Oxfam does not necessarily endorse any text or activities that accompany the materials, nor has it approved the adapted text.

have power and resources to do more to solve environmental problems, and b) they have the capacity to make it easier and less costly for individuals to act in environmentally friendly ways."[23] Wealthy individuals in particular are much more able to have an impact. The chart in figure 2 comes from the aptly titled blog post "The Best Way to Reduce Your Personal Carbon Emissions: Don't Be Rich."

The author of the blog post, David Roberts, explains: "The choices of developed-world citizens matter more than the choices of (say) Chinese citizens, and the choices of wealthy developed-world citizens matter most of all. The rich, in other words [the top 10 percent], are the ones that should be getting hassled about their choices. For most working schmoes, this kind of moralizing of lifestyle is as pointless as it is off-putting." Then he adds that "climate change simply does not fit well in the individual choices frame."[24] But who are these top 10 percent? We want to believe it is only the rich businessmen who fly from New York to London once a week and that the rest of us are the "working schmoes." Yet compared to the rest of the world, a middle-class American with modest assets may be quite privileged. To be one of the richest top 10 percent in the world in 2016, according to Ana Swanson, writing for the *Washington Post* "Wonkblog," one needed only $68,000 in wealth.[25] Another study defined "the world's wealthiest individuals" as "those owning over $100,000 in assets." This group totals 8.6 percent of the global population but owns 85.6 percent of global wealth.[26] We can fight about the exact numbers. The point is that many of us in the United States, including perhaps David Roberts, may think we are "working schmoes," but we actually are among the richest 10 percent in the world. We are privileged, and our choices about our carbon footprints matter. I agree that the rich are the ones we should hassle about their lifestyle choices, but that group may include you and me.

The old idea about "common but differentiated responsibilities and respective capabilities," a central principle within the U.N. Framework Convention on Climate Change, may be even more relevant for thinking about the capabilities and responsibilities of individual people and groups than it is about the responsibilities of countries. This principle was used to justify the idea that developing countries, which historically had less responsibility for emissions, should not be subject to concrete emissions goals under the Kyoto Agreement. Under the Paris Agreement, however, all countries set voluntary goals. This is consistent with a forward-looking model of responsibility, which is focused not on who is to blame but on all those socially connected to a structural injustice who are capable of taking action. But the idea that "respective capabilities" should contribute to differentiated responsibilities is still relevant in the sense that those with more power, privilege, and collective ability need to take their choices about responsible action most seriously.

The importance of including all countries in a forward-looking responsibility model becomes clearer when we look at the corporations that are most responsible for emissions. One study suggests that one hundred companies are responsible for 71 percent of global emissions.[27] These include many fossil-fuel producers, including state-owned companies. Of course, it is difficult to apportion responsibility consistently for production and consumption, and the responsibility of fossil-fuel, mining, and refining companies is particularly difficult to calculate because it is not clear if they are responsible only for their mining and extractive activities or for the emissions from burning the fuel as well. It is ultimately consumers who use the electricity and transportation, including freight transport, powered by those fuels. If holding parents responsible for their children's emissions is a category error, the same is true of holding fossil-fuel producers responsible for all the energy their fuels generate, instead of attributing it to the consumers who demand and use it. Even so, we can learn something interesting from this study. Aside from the usual developed-world suspects like Exxon/Mobile and Shell, the top ten companies generating greenhouse gases include two from China, two from Russia, and one each from Saudi Arabia, Iran, India, and Mexico. In other words, while wealthy individuals, mainly located in the developed world, are largely responsible for lifestyle consumption emissions, the responsibility for industrial emissions is more spread out. A single sector in a single country—Chinese coal—accounts for 14.3 percent of cumulative emissions from 1988 through 2015, dwarfing the contributions of all other sources.

We need to be much more fine-grained when we talk about responsibility for climate change. Casual generalizations that "industry, not humans, are responsible" or that "climate change simply does not fit well in the individual choices frame" do not capture this complexity. And they discourage people from trying to make a positive difference when industry, governments, institutions, and individuals all need to be part of the solution.

DEFENSE AGAINST THE DARK ARTS: DIGITAL PRIVACY AND DISINFORMATION

After my op-ed, "Wake Up Hapless Technology Users," was published, my friend and colleague Steven Livingston invited me to a technology conference in Washington, D.C., entitled "Contentious Narratives: Digital Technology and the Attacks on Liberal Democratic Norms." I felt like one of the hapless technology users I described, sneaking into an expert meeting. Panelists at the conference pointed to sophisticated new strategies being used to mislead and manipulate the public, distort elections, and hide human rights violations. The panelists framed these as technically complex issues, requiring technical fixes that could barely be understood, much less implemented, by mere mortals. They emphasized state and corporate responsibility. I completely agree on the importance of state and corporate accountability. Legislatures in countries around the world need to pass legislation regulating social media companies so that they are more transparent and accountable. Social media companies, for example, should disclose bots on their platforms and prohibit candidates and parties from using bots. It may be important for social media to restrict content at times, but they should also be expected to clarify the criteria they use to restrict content and to open their algorithms and data to outside scrutiny, either through review boards or other mechanisms.[28]

But if our democracies are to have more resilience against digital threats, it is not sufficient for just governments and corporations to take action. Societal groups, including NGOs, universities, professors, and students, must exercise responsibilities as well. There are simple steps people in the broader community can take not only to protect their own privacy, but also to protect the privacy of others and to help secure our democracies from disinformation and manipulation through social media platforms.

We will all need more training. This training is sometimes called "digital hygiene," but we have to find a better name because "digital hygiene" sounds too much like brushing one's teeth. A better metaphor would be a vaccination: when one opts out, one imposes an external cost on others.

People who do not install anti-virus software, for example, are more likely to be recruited for a botnet and endanger others.[29] At the conference, another participant and I began brainstorming about training young people, and we decided the training should be called "Defense against the Digital Dark Arts," in homage to Harry Potter. After hearing about all the ways that sketchy and dangerous actors are using digital disinformation to manipulate us and our political system, we decided that there are indeed dark arts in the digital world. The grown-ups of the world (governments and corporations) need to put up a strong defense against them. But just as in Harry Potter's world, grown-ups cannot defend against every attack, and even the less experienced are drawn into the fray.

At the end of the conference, I spoke on a panel on remedies to some of the technological problems we had examined. I argued that we need new norms and practices of responsibility surrounding digital privacy and disinformation and that in order to achieve new norms, we often require some shock that wakes people up and forces them to pay attention. The shock turns what seemed to be an individual choice into a collective issue. It was very difficult, for example, to change the norms about smoking as long as it was simply a matter of adults doing stupid things to their own bodies. The research on passive smoke turned the debate around; once the issue became the harm smokers did to the bodies of those around them, smokers' responsibilities increased.

In the wake of the Cambridge Analytica scandal in 2018, digital privacy may be reaching its passive smoke moment. Earlier hacking scandals, such as that of Yahoo in 2013 and Equinox in 2017, were clearly problems with corporate irresponsibility and the failure of corporations to protect their customers. The Cambridge Analytica hack called into question Facebook's policies, but it also highlighted the responsibility of individual Facebook users. When two hundred thousand individuals on Facebook did something careless—they took a survey that in turn downloaded an app—they imperiled the privacy of perhaps eighty-seven million other unsuspecting Facebook users when the app scraped their contacts. Individual actions as well as corporate ones have the potential to put people at risk.

For the time being, technology companies expect consumers to take responsibility for their privacy. Adam Conner, founder of Facebook's Washington, D.C., office and most recently working for Slack Technologies, explained that when an individual installs an app that wants to access that person's contact book, a little pop-up appears and asks for access to it. The answer can be "OK" or "Don't allow." Conner went on: "Is there an argument to be made that maybe you should have more information about what that means, that your addresses, everything in your address book, is now going to go to somebody else's machine to be used in perpetuity until you reach out and delete it? There's an argument, but the flip side is, you're a smart person, you know your contacts are doing that, and you're clicking okay, so, you know, in that scenario maybe it's okay."[30]

The conference's keynote address was given by General James Clapper, the director of national intelligence during the Obama administration. General Clapper told us that 90 percent of the cyberattacks his staff faced were spear-phishing attacks aimed at individuals. Spear phishing, I learned, is like phishing in that it is an effort to obtain unauthorized access to sensitive information. A spear-phishing email, however, targets a specific individual or organization and appears to come from a trusted source, perhaps even someone in one's contact list. Presumably hostile foreign countries were the sources of these attacks in national security agencies. But many of the spear-phishing attacks that show up in our work and personal email come from criminal groups trying to gain access to our financial information. Here we have no Facebook to blame for the scandal, as in the Cambridge Analytica affair. The attacks come over ordinary email, and we have no line of defense except our spam system and our own good sense. Even Clapper's highly trained intelligence staff often clicked the links or opened attachments that activated attacks. The famous release of John Podesta's Democratic National Committee emails came from a spear-phishing attack. Given the difficulty that institutions have in keeping pace with technology, we cannot wait for corporate or state policy changes; individuals and organizations must change their norms and practices. We need security awareness and training, what some at the conference called "digital civics." By learning how to detect spear phishing, ordinary people can begin to take some responsibility for their digital privacy.

The role of individuals may be even more important in the area of "fake news" and disinformation than in digital privacy. Russian use of social media to manipulate U.S. elections started with a foreign power but was multiplied by individuals retweeting Russian bots, forwarding email, or posting fake news on their Facebook pages. This is happening not only in the United States. In the Brazilian elections in 2018, the election of right-wing president Jair Bolsonaro was propelled by the spread of disinformation on social media, especially through WhatsApp.

Although President Trump uses the term "fake news" to describe any unfavorable (to him) news story, it is also "an analytical term that describes deliberate disinformation presented in the form of a conventional news report."[31] Fake news is not new, but it has recently accelerated, in large part because two-thirds of American adults get some of their news from social media platforms, many of which lend themselves to the spread of disinformation.[32] But because much diffusion of disinformation is the result of individuals retweeting, posting, and forwarding the news, we are not completely helpless in this context. Individuals and educational institutions, for example, can take actions to diminish the spread of disinformation.

Fake news is the epitome of a decentralized problem where the concept of human rights doesn't take us very far. Human rights commentators and international human rights bodies have accepted that we have a "right to information," usually based on our right to freedom of expression.[33] But none of these rights gets to the core of the problem with fake news. Presumably we have a right to "accurate information," but the stress has always been the freedom to individual expression, neutral with regard to content, including what we would call fake news. In other words, in general the spread of fake news by individuals is protected by human rights unless it is libel or slander or, in some countries, but not the United States, hate speech. The problem with fake news is that too little attention is paid to the responsibility to have some factual basis for free expression. This is properly in the arena of ethical and political responsibilities, not legal ones. The possibility of state manipulation of legal liability for factual speech is all too apparent. But complete citizen irresponsibility with regard to the spreading of lies is equally troublesome.

This problem is in the wheelhouse of educators, but we have been slow to step up to the challenge of fake news. Teachers of history and social science have long stressed the importance of using reliable sources. The task of teaching about fake news is related, but it is less about footnoting good sources and more about the responsibilities of citizens in spreading ideas. If you are uncertain about whether the information comes from a trusted source, you should not be using it or spreading it. Preferably you should not be "liking" it either. While President Trump's actions have called our attention to these issues, this needs to be a non-partisan training program about responsible research and citizenship, not focused on any political leader or party.

We can't leave these responsibilities to educational institutions; we need to stress them as well in our personal interactions with friends and family. One close friend of mine, for example, finally pushed back against his dad, who kept forwarding him fake news stories. He told his dad that he had to check the accuracy of the story before he forwarded it. And his dad eventually followed his suggestion. My friend and his father still don't agree about politics, but they were able to agree about certain basic procedures that should be taken before forwarding an email.

My remarks at the conference drew a fair amount of skepticism. Many felt that focusing on technology users' responsibilities was beside the point or completely inadequate. But if universities paid nearly as much attention to digital privacy rights as they do to the rights of human research subjects, we would be far ahead of most of our society. I had to go through a three-month process of application and training to guarantee the privacy of about forty undergraduates when I asked them to participate in focus groups on voting for this book (see chapter 5). But few universities are training faculty or students in any serious digital defense against the dark arts—how to take precautions to protect their own privacy online or on social media platforms. The IT services of universities work hard to protect against spam and data breaches. They oblige us to change our passwords frequently and require dual-factor authentication to log onto accounts. We need to help them more and not see their efforts only as a nuisance. After years of resisting constant attempts to force us to switch passwords, I'm finally complying and even using dual-factor authentication on my work computer, my home computer, and my phone, despite the bother. We need the universities also to step forward and require online and hands-on training, such as how to avoid spear-phishing attacks and how to distinguish disinformation from trusted sources online.

HOW TO AVOID OBLIGATIONS

Iris Young mentions several rhetorical strategies for avoiding responsibility that correspond to what I have encountered in my discussions and other reading. All of them appear in both everyday and scholarly discussions of responsibilities for climate change and digital privacy. The four main strategies Young identified are the following:

GLOBAL RIGHTS & RESPONSIBILITIES

(1) Reification, or treating products of human action "as if they are things or natural forces";

(2) Denying one's connection to a structural injustice because one is not to blame for it;

(3) Using our obligations to the persons with whom we interact every day to distract us from our obligations to distant others; and

(4) "Not my job."[34]

All these strategies have been used by otherwise thoughtful and committed actors in the two main issues discussed above.

Another way of thinking about reification is in the terms of structural versus agentic accounts of politics. Reification often depends on a structural view of political life in which powerful forces beyond our control shape politics and we have little power to change it. Reification is common in the area of digital privacy. People see many features of social media as inevitable. Consumers accept that social media outlets willfully produce lies as if this were natural. But a responsibility view requires that we acknowledge that digital privacy or the lack of it is a product of human action and, as such, can and should be altered by human action.

Denying a connection to a structural injustice is also common. For example, David Roberts, the blogger who argued that the rich should be hassled for their consumption choices but that moralizing to "working schmoes" is pointless and off-putting, appears to identify himself as a working man and thus to deny his connection to climate change. Most people who say that they don't care about their digital privacy and therefore don't need to understand their devices' privacy settings are likewise denying connection.

The immediacy of other obligations is the rhetorical strategy for which I have the most sympathy. Because people have pressing obligations to family, community, and work, they may feel they are too busy to worry about complex and distant problems like climate change or digital privacy. Even the thought of dealing with these issues leaves them feeling overwhelmed and confused. Thus it is very helpful and important when experts give us clear, simple solutions supported by research. I was very grateful to Gidon Eshel, for example, for listing the one simple but effective food decision we could make to address climate change. I didn't have time to sort through all the literature, but I trusted his expertise and was prepared to stop buying and eating beef as a result.

I have found, however, that the most common rhetorical strategy for avoiding responsibility is the fourth: "Not my job." This is the claim of individuals or other non-state actors that they should not be expected to take action to protect rights. Among the most common of these arguments is the one that says, "It's the government's job."[35] Some people think that if individuals step forward to take responsibilities for some public-policy issue that governments "should take," we will start on a slippery slope to letting governments evade their responsibilities. Once, while I was driving in Minnesota with a friend from Uruguay, we saw a sign announcing that the Rotary Club had taken responsibility for cleaning up a two-mile stretch of the highway. My friend said that she hated those signs because ridding the highways of garbage was the state's job. I remember being shocked at the time and arguing with her. The litter on the highway came almost entirely from one source: individual drivers who threw stuff out their windows. Nothing was more salutary in my mind than seeing the Rotary Club members out on a Saturday afternoon with their children, clearing up the roadside. Maybe those children would think twice before throwing a candy wrapper out the window. In this case, the municipal or county government is often responsible for cutting the roadside grass, building fences, and generally keeping the area clean, but it cannot do it properly as long as people keep throwing trash from their cars.

Municipal governments are also responsible for placing receptacles at roadside stops to make it easy to throw away garbage. Once it is in the receptacle, a government employee is supposed to pick it up for disposal. Yet the fulfillment of this responsibility is not always so simple. I remember my friend Sue from Gloucester telling me about garbage on the Good Harbor Beach. The city put out garbage bins, but on a good beach day they were invariably overfilled by early afternoon. People would then pile their trash next to the receptacles instead of taking it away when they left, and some of that piled garbage would blow into the sea. In response, the city took away the trash bins, and the beach is now cleaner because people accept that they have a responsibility to pack out everything that they packed onto the beach. Still, when Sue walks on the beach every morning, she takes a plastic bag with her and fills it with garbage people have left behind. She believes the cleanliness of the beach has become everyone's business and responsibility. We therefore must simultaneously be concerned about state and individual responsibility, both for ethical reasons and for the sometimes surprising and counterintuitive efficacy that determined assertion of individual responsibility can have.

Yet another rhetorical argument against responsibility, not mentioned by Young, is the "either-or" or "crowding out" argument: people can do only one thing or another, and attention to individual responsibility prevents them from doing other things, including working with others. One of my colleagues suggested that too much focus on individual responsibility, especially in an individualistic society like that of the United States, can "soak up all the air," which is another version of the crowding out argument.[36] Shortly after the Cambridge Analytica scandal, technology expert Siva Vaidhyanathan published an op-ed article entitled "Don't Delete Facebook. Do Something about It." He argues that it does not make a difference to Facebook or to the state of the world if you delete or suspend your Facebook account. Instead, he argues, quitting Facebook "lets Google and Twitter off the hook. It lets AT&T and Comcast and its peers off the hook. . . . If we act as disconnected, indignant moral agents, we surrender the only power we have: the power to think and act collectively."[37]

While Vaidhyanathan is right that people need to think and act collectively, he is wrong to suggest that people who are motivated to delete Facebook might thus "surrender" their ability to act collectively. By deleting your Facebook account, you don't surrender the ability to act collectively. People both on and off Facebook are equally able to act together as citizens to regulate corporations. There is no evidence that people who take individual actions in, for example, either the environment or digital privacy are less likely than others to

GLOBAL RIGHTS & RESPONSIBILITIES

act collectively. In fact, there is a good reason to believe that people who recycle and turn off lights at home are more likely to organize at work or in their communities around climate change—or to support the efforts of others. Those who take time to understand their personal digital privacy situations are more likely to be alarmed and try to organize with others to provide privacy. Do people really think that if we spend a half hour turning on privacy protections, we might not sign a petition condemning Facebook's actions or join a class-action lawsuit against the company? Taking responsibility in one domain in no way precludes taking responsibility in others.

CHAPTER FOUR

National Rights and Responsibilities: Voting

T HE need to promote new norms and practices of networked responsibility is nowhere more pressing than in the area of voting. The need is especially urgent among the young, whose turnout is very weak. It is hard to argue for a responsibility to vote without arguing for a corresponding responsibility to inform oneself in order to vote; yet while college students vote in smaller numbers than the general population, they are well placed to be informed about elections. They live in an environment where they can easily get good information from classes, professors, libraries, civil society organizations, and fellow students. Most college students are also people with options and collective ability. They are either part of privileged segments of society or trying to enter those segments. As such, they fit the parameters Iris Young finds most eligible to be part of networked responsibility.[1]

In 1976, as part of an undergraduate exchange program, I spent a year in Uruguay, during the darkest days of its dictatorship. I was saddened by what I learned about human rights while living in Uruguay, yet puzzled. How could one of the oldest democracies in the Americas, mainly democratic since the turn of the century, have succumbed to a military coup in 1973, along with Chile, South America's other great democracy? The most persuasive explanations for the breakdown focused on beliefs, norms, and practices that are essential to sustaining and protecting democracy. Juan Linz, for example, writing about the breakdown of democratic regimes in Europe and Latin America in the mid-twentieth century, stressed the importance of beliefs in the rise and fall of democracy, particularly beliefs about the legitimacy of democracy itself.[2] For Linz, what made an institution legitimate was not that it was the best system one could imagine but that it was seen as better than any other institution that could be established. This is a similar point to the well-known statement by Winston Churchill: "Democracy is the worst form of government except for all those other forms that have been tried from time to time."[3]

Linz argued that intellectuals play a major role in "formulating, elaborating, and transmitting" ideas about legitimacy.[4] In Latin America in the 1970s, intellectuals and social movements on both the left and the right contributed to the delegitimation of democracy. Mainwaring and Pérez-Liñán's book, *Democracies and Dictatorships in Latin America*, the definitive work on this topic, concluded that people's beliefs and the international context are the most important factors associated with democratic stability. They find that democracy failed in Latin America in part because people stopped believing in it.[5] This view seems simple, maybe even obvious, but it runs contrary to the arguments of many political scientists, who often do not take beliefs seriously.

It is not only the elites whose attitudes matter for protecting democracy. The ideas and practices of ordinary people matter as well. Elizabeth Jelin argues that a sustained democracy requires a "culture of citizenship from below." This culture of citizenship must be about both rights and responsibilities, including but going far beyond the responsibility to vote.[6]

Why did people in Latin America stop believing in democracy, and what made them start believing again? The reasons are complex, but an answer to the first question is that democracy, as practiced in Latin America, fell far short of people's ideals. Leftists dreamed of a more participatory and egalitarian system and disdained "bourgeois democracy," which they saw as a pale substitute.[7] As leftists became convinced that they would never be allowed to come to power through elections, they focused on armed struggle. Rightists preferred military regimes to what they perceived as chaotic democracies. The resulting military regimes engaged in levels of repression and violence not seen in most Latin American countries since the colonial period.

I worry that lack of belief in voting in the United States could lead us down the same path because it suggests that people no longer value or engage in the crucial practices of democracy. When I see the arguments for violence being made by some activists from "Antifa" (short for militant Anti-fascists), I do not see them as new and revolutionary but as familiar and dangerous. When I see social movements of both

the left and right contributing to such extensive delegitimation of the state that it becomes an act of political protest
not to vote, it reminds me of how Latin Americans stopped
believing in democracy. So I was encouraged when I learned
the ways in which students at Harvard not only affirmed
their belief in democracy, but also worked to expand voter
participation on campus.

VOTER PARTICIPATION IN THE UNITED STATES

In May 2018, the Harvard Kennedy School (HKS) held an
all-day conference on increasing voter turnout in the United
States. The "moonshot" goal was to raise U.S. turnout to 80
percent.[8] Since the turnout in Minnesota, the highest in the
country, reached 74 percent in the 2016 presidential election,
the 80 percent goal does not seem outlandish. Organized by
long-time voting guru Miles Rapoport and the HKS's own
Teresa Acuña, the conference brought together amazing people engaged in and committed to voting. Participants included the secretaries of state of Colorado and Minnesota, two
states at the cutting edge of innovations to enhance voting;
private-sector actors working to promote voter turnout, such
as Tumblr, Google, and Patagonia; and civil society organizations mobilizing non-voters, such as the Civic Engagement
Fund, the Electoral Justice Project, and LIBRE Initiative.

Peter Levine, from Tufts University's Tisch College of
Civic Life, also attended. In a blog he produced to accompany
the conference, Levine provided two charts to put the 80 percent goal in historical context. The first graph (figure 3) shows

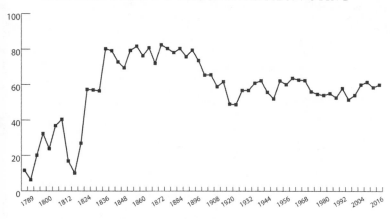

Figure 3: U.S. presidential election turnout as percentage
of eligible voters, 1789–2016.

Source: United States Elections Project, "National General Election VEP
Turnout Rates, 1789–Present," June 11, 2014 (http://www.electproject.org/
national-1789-present).

the percentage of eligible voters who voted in presidential elections. The peaks of that graph, around 80 percent, came in the mid- to late 1800s, when only white men could vote. The graph's next-to-final data point is from 2012, when all citizens eighteen years and older, except some with felony convictions, were eligible to vote. In this much larger pool, just under 60 percent of eligible voters voted in presidential elections. The challenge we face is therefore not getting "back" to 80 percent but how to achieve that level of turnout in an environment of greater enfranchisement.[9]

The second graph (figure 4) shows the dramatic expansion of enfranchised voters in the United States—that is, the voter turnout as a fraction of the total U.S. population.

Figure 4: U.S. popular vote for president as
fraction of total population, 1788–2012.

Data compiled from *Encyclopaedia Britannica*
(https://www.britannica.com/topic/United-States-
Presidential-Election-Results-1788863).

The most recently incorporated group is young people
aged 18–20, who received the right to vote in 1971. About 40
percent of people aged 18–24 are in college, so looking at college
student turnout tells us a lot about voter participation among
the latest group of enfranchised voters. In recent years we have
had excellent data on college voting patterns. Since 2012, the
Institute for Democracy and Higher Education at Tufts University has produced the National Study of Learning, Voting, and
Engagement, or NSLVE. NSLVE collects data on the voting
practices of almost ten million college students in over one
thousand institutions across all fifty states, including undergraduates, graduate students, and non-traditional students.[10]

According to NSLVE data, college student turnout in
2016 was two points lower than that of youth voters (18–29)
and twelve points lower than the overall turnout of eligible
voters. Nevertheless, voter turnout among eligible college stu-

dents increased in presidential elections from 2012 to 2016 by about three percentage points, from 45.1 percent to 48.3 percent, and among the youngest group of college students (those aged 18–21) there was a 4 percent increase. This is important because voting is a habit: once people do it, they are more likely to vote in the future, so it makes sense to develop the habit early in life.[11] College voter turnout for midterm elections is much lower. The average voting rate for all college students was 18 percent in midterm elections in 2014. For students aged 18–21, the number was even smaller: 13 percent. There is fascinating variation in all of these patterns. Women students vote more than men, students in the Northeast and Midwest vote more than those in the Southwest, and social science majors vote more than those in STEM fields (science, technology, engineering, and mathematics). Private institutions have higher voting rates, but this may be entirely due to their students' socioeconomic status since affluent people, students included, are more likely to vote than poor people.

But there is also variation among institutions with similar student bodies. College voting increased by as much as 15 percent at some institutions between 2012 and 2016. NSLVE staffers conducted qualitative research, including focus groups on campuses and other forms of in-depth engagement, to find out what such institutions and their students and faculty did that caused such dramatic increases. Preliminary research leads them to conclude, tentatively, that "campus climates—the norms, structures, behaviors, and attitudes of people on campuses—can influence student decisions whether or not to vote or to be otherwise politically engaged. ... We hypothesize that pervasive political discussions, strong faculty-student relationships coupled with political learning across disciplines, and vibrant electoral activities are attributes of a robust campus climate for political engagement."[12]

The NSLVE director, Nancy Thomas, confirmed the importance of "underlying norms" and "creating a campus climate or a campus culture" leading to high voter turnout. Faculty, students, and administrators all have a role in creating and sustaining these norms, which are completely in tune with these institutions' purposes. Universities often have "civic engagement" as part of their mission statement. Harvard College's mission, for example, is to "educate the citizens and citizen-leaders for our society."[13] Voting is a simple but important type of engagement.

INCREASING VOTER TURNOUT AT HARVARD

Just under half (48.5 percent) of Harvard students voted in the presidential elections of 2012, slightly higher than the average level of student voting in the country.[14] In the 2016 elections, 57.8 percent of Harvard students voted, 9.3 points higher than their turnout in 2012, and 7.4 points higher than the average of all other institutions for which NSLVE has data.[15]

What happened at Harvard between 2012 and 2016 to raise student voter turnout? The network behind the changes included a nonprofit startup, TurboVote; students from the Community Action Committee (CAC) of Harvard's Institute of Politics (IOP); the IOP leaders and staff; and the university's leaders and technical staff. This case illustrates that there are many ways for actors to exercise responsibility and that individual actions have an impact on larger outcomes.

The story begins in 2010, when three HKS students (Seth Flaxman, Kathryn Peters, and Amanda Cassel Kraft) set out to build a reminder system for upcoming elections so that students would not forget to vote. As a graduate student living away from home, Flaxman had missed several elections, so he understood the difficulties students faced. He said, "If an Ivy League graduate student obsessed with voting is missing three elections in a row, there has got to be a process problem."[16] He found he was not alone: "Sixty-six percent of students in 2010 said they didn't vote because they were either busy, working, or had forgotten."[17] Flaxman looked online for a service that would give him information and reminders on voting and found it didn't exist. So Flaxman, Peters, and Kraft co-founded a nonprofit group called Democracy Works and launched their first project, TurboVote, an online service to help U.S. citizens register and vote. Their idea was to make voting as easy as ordering movies from Netflix. They received early funding from the Google Election Center and the Sunlight Foundation, adding the private sector and foundations into the network of agents taking responsibility for voter turnout.[18] Flaxman explained, "The majority of Americans can vote by mail, but the process is terrible. . . . You have to go to three different government websites: one to get a form, another to get an address, and then a third to figure out a deadline. And the deadline is usually three Thursdays before an election day that you don't remember. We take out those steps."[19] Users who need to register by mail receive completed forms with an envelope already stamped and addressed. Users who opt in get text and email reminders with important election information, key dates, and deadlines.[20] The program automatically tracks their hometown election calendars and sends them updates on everything from local school-board elections to primaries to presidential elections.[21]

The Community Action Committee

Harvard College was one of TurboVote's earliest university partners. Harvard's IOP was established in 1966 to engage students, particularly undergraduates, to consider careers in politics and public service. One of the IOP's programs is the CAC, a student committee that works to bridge the gap between politics and public service through targeted service projects on campus and in the greater Boston area.[22] The IOP had been conducting voter registration on campus since 1999, and these activities eventually fell under CAC's umbrella.

In the fall of 2014, when Austin Sowa was a freshman and a new member of the CAC, he and other students associated with the program decided to revitalize voter registration on campus. Sowa, who was chairman of the organization in 2015–16, believes deeply that voting is a duty, a responsibility, and a privilege. He was "very much worried about the lack of accessibility of voter registration at Harvard."[23] Over the next two years, Sowa and the CAC students worked with IOP staff to transform CAC from a general community service organization to one focused on "improving voter registration right here in our own community at Harvard," using TurboVote technology to develop on-the-ground registration efforts on campus.[24] At that time, Harvard had a "Study Card Day" at the beginning of each semester, when every student had to go to University Hall to sign up for classes. Since all the students would be bottlenecked in the same place, Sowa and his fellow students set up tables in the hallway, where students could register to vote using the TurboVote software. They also held a rally at the Science Plaza on campus for National Voter Registration Day, where they not only registered students to vote, but also had music, volunteers in costumes, and candy. By the end of 2014 the CAC had helped to register seven hundred students. "That's not an insignificant number," Sowa pointed out, but "we were missing thousands of people, and we just didn't have enough time."[25]

In 2015, Harvard digitized Study Card Day, leaving CAC without a place to encounter every student on the same day. "We had to come up with a new strategy to fit this new context," said Sowa. "I remember thinking there must be an easier way. We needed to make it more accessible and efficient. We were focusing so much on registering people that we were not educating them and we were not mobilizing them."[26]

Sowa proposed that the IOP fold voter registration into the mandatory online check-in completed by all undergraduates when they arrive on campus; it could be done simply by adding a TurboVote link. By this time he was vice president of the student executive committee of the IOP, and he and IOP executive director Catherine McLaughlin pitched the idea to the university registrar who managed the undergraduate check-in process. Because the college values student leadership, Sowa and McLaughlin stressed that this was a student idea, as well as that the U.S. Higher Education Act obligates the college to "make a good faith effort" to distribute voter registration forms.[27] Under the CAC proposal, voter registration itself would remain voluntary, but it would become more visible and easier to access.[28]

The registrar approved the plan, as did other Harvard officials, including President Drew Faust. Faust, who had likened TurboVote to "drive-in voting," commented that "a liberal-arts education is meant to educate people in a variety of ways, and I think one of those ways is the responsibility to vote."[29]

Harvard's IT staff worked with TurboVote to implement CAC's plan. Together, the entire networked group of CAC, the IOP, TurboVote, the registrar's office, and the IT staff put the institution at the cutting edge of higher education voter registration.[30] They made registering to vote easier for undergraduates, although those students still had to choose to do it and to vote. For each student who registers for mail-in or absentee voting in a state that requires a signed paper sent by regular mail, TurboVote prints and delivers the ballot to the student's mailbox with a stamped and addressed envelope. Harvard pays for the envelopes and stamps so that students have only to sign the form, place it in the envelope, and mail it.

The first implementation of this online strategy, in 2015, resulted in nearly fourteen hundred undergraduates signing up for TurboVote during check-in—twice as many as Sowa's group had managed to register in the fall of 2014. While this effort was unarguably a success, this figure represented only one in four Harvard undergraduates. About 10 percent were international and not eligible to vote. What about the others? Were they already registered? Were they uncertain if they had already registered? Or did they just not want to register to vote?

Simply signing up with TurboVote doesn't complete voter registration in all cases. Some states required signed forms, which TurboVote promised to send. In focus groups I conducted in 2018, Harvard students were not shy about discussing TurboVote's failings. At times, they said, the promised forms did not arrive, and by the time they realized this, the deadline for registering to vote absentee had already passed.

Nor do registration numbers necessarily tell us about voter turnout. The campaign focused only on voter registration, which did increase at Harvard. There was also a big increase in Harvard student voter turnout between the 2012 presidential election and that of 2016, but we do not know the exact reasons for it. But because Harvard voting levels were significantly higher than the average college level, the technical fix of adding TurboVote to the check-in was likely part of the explanation.

The voter registration campaign at Harvard involved a network of diverse non-state actors who acknowledged their responsibilities to vote and to help others vote and then worked together to motivate a community of almost seven thousand students to exercise that right despite the imperfect and difficult system of voter registration in the United States. All the students' actions were discretionary. No one told them what they should do; rather, they forged their own path and recruited support along the way. The students felt a deep sense of responsibility and possibility, and they themselves decided what actions to take to fulfill this responsibility.

What was oddly missing from the TurboVote campaign was any meaningful role for faculty. Nancy Thomas argues, "Faculty are critical to voter turn-out" on campus, and "Faculty often have no idea how important they are to students."[31] Yet in the interviews my assistants and I conducted for this chapter, Harvard faculty were rarely mentioned. We asked the current co-chair of CAC, Derek Paulhus—a government major—whether his professors had talked in class about the responsibility to vote. He answered, "No not really, and that's kind of a sad thing. ... It's more of a political science approach, like these groups vote for this because of this, or this party attracts these voters because of this. It's never about 'This is how to mobilize voters.' I've never been exposed to anything like that in the Gov department."[32]

Harvard students and staff also shared their experience with other schools, hoping to scale up the initiative. Nevertheless, as we will see in the next chapter, there was still much work to be done, especially in encouraging voter turnout. Focus groups I conducted with Harvard undergraduates in the spring of 2018 suggested that most students believe in the responsibility to vote, but many still feel voting is situational and optional, and that it remains confusing and difficult.

CHAPTER FIVE

What Do the Students Think?

AFTER learning about the CAC campaign for student voter registration, I became curious about what students at Harvard feel about voting, especially about whether they believe they have a responsibility to vote.[1] In the spring of 2018, my research assistants and I invited Harvard undergraduates to join a series of focus groups to discuss their attitudes about voting.[2] I made it clear I did not want to discuss who they voted for but what they thought about voting as a practice. We promised them complete confidentiality.

Some may think that Harvard undergrads are a fairly homogeneous group, but we found significant diversity along many lines, including their attitudes. It is possible that we attracted students more interested in voting than the average Harvard undergraduate, but the students certainly did not all speak with one voice. I did not ask them their political affiliations, but a few volunteered that they identified as conservatives, making clear that the groups were not composed only of liberal students. We had good gender balance and a variety of areas of study, with students representing all four years and all regions of the country. We even had a few international students. A number of participants were the first-generation children of immigrants, and representation of racial and ethnic minorities was higher than in the Harvard undergraduate population as a whole.

The students were articulate and meandering, moving and trivial, and occasionally funny and ironic. They disagreed with one another easily and without obvious tension or conflict. A number of the seniors said their first political memory came in the aftermath of the election of 2000, with someone, usually a parent, trying to explain why the individual who got the most votes didn't win the election or why a ballot particularity like hanging chads in a single county might swing an entire national election. Their earliest memories of voting are thus connected to problems with the U.S. voting system, and they learned at a young age to view voting as complicated at best and unfair and illegitimate at worst.

A RESPONSIBILITY TO VOTE?

Every group contained at least one person who clearly articulated the belief that one has an absolute responsibility to vote. One student said, "Citizenship is a privilege that comes with specific duties, one of which is to participate in governance in a republican system."[3] Another said, "It's a privilege to live in a democracy . . . and if you're going to take advantage of the benefits that come with living in an established society, you have an obligation to contribute to it, and voting is the most direct way that we have to do that."[4] But students also pointed out the many difficulties people in the United States face when they try to vote. As one concluded, "If you want to talk about voting being sort of an obligation for an American citizen, then I think you also have to have the conversation of how you can make that feasible."[5]

A few students argued that there was no responsibility to vote and that there might, in fact, be good reasons not to vote. One student said his roommate had told him, "There is no personal incentive that would get [him] to vote." "As much as I was discouraged to hear the answer," the student continued, "I sort of had to agree with him because I think, on the face of it, the difference between you before casting the vote and after is not much, besides maybe self-esteem."[6] Another said, "I come from a community that's very independent-minded, and people actively choose not to vote. It's a very active and political decision to not vote because they don't believe in the system, and they don't want to endorse it."[7] Said another, "I'm really into this movement called the New Monasticism, by this guy named Shane Claiborne, who vocally does not vote for a set of civil disobedience reasons."[8]

Most students fell between these two positions, arguing that voting is the right thing to do but that it is optional and situational and that there are many reasons why it might be acceptable not to vote. While they articulated this position in terms of responsibility, their arguments revealed that it was not a responsibility they took seriously. Some thought that voting is only for those who have strong political beliefs: "If you want to make your voice heard, then you have a responsibility to vote, but I don't know if just by living in a particular county or country, you have an innate responsibility to vote; maybe you just don't care enough."[9] A number commented that one has a responsibility to vote if one wants to complain about politics. Yet another argued that political responsibility "is not restricted to voting. I think it's up to you to decide how you want to contribute to civic life. If you want to volunteer, that's great; if you want to vote, that's great; if you want to do some other political work, that's also great. It's your choice."[10]

Many students pointed out that at least in some parts of the United States, one's vote does not matter, and this absolves one of the responsibility to vote. A student stressed that "a lot of people want to vote, but they don't because they feel like their vote doesn't matter. It feels like voting only matters in some states. . . . We have to address the facts that sometimes the act of voting is just formality, so we have to focus on the things we can do, and if voting isn't something we can do to enact change, then we have to find something else."[11] In a different group, a student noted, "The people I know who don't vote . . . they feel a lack of efficacy."[12]

A number of students believed that people who are not well informed do not have a responsibility to vote. One said, "I'm not sure if I want people who are self-admittedly uninformed filling out ballots, so maybe it shouldn't be seen as a mandatory civic duty to vote just for the sake of voting if you don't have a serious opinion."[13] This was not simply an elitist opinion; several students doubted whether they or their fellow students had enough information to vote.

One student summed up an issue that is at the heart of this book in simple language: how to combine advocacy with attention to individual responsibility. "I think there are two things that the average student can do. One would be keep working on their personal voting habits because not everyone votes in every election—like I've missed municipal elections. . . . It's not anybody else's fault, but I just forget that I have to mail it in at a certain time, and I said, 'Oops, that's my fault.' And so personal responsibility is not a binary; it's something you continue to cultivate. And then the other part is advocacy, but that's a much higher bar; there are undergrads that are currently going to go lobby Congress about specific things."[14]

I love the language here: first to conceive of responsibility and advocacy as complementary, then to think of personal responsibility as "something you continue to cultivate"—even as you admit that you sometimes fail to meet your goals and need to say, "Oops, that's my fault."

VOTING AS COMPLEX AND DIFFICULT

For many people in our society, including the young, voting is difficult and complicated. Many students in the focus groups said it was hard and confusing. One freshman from Tennessee was getting ready to vote for the first time after arriving at college. "For some reason, Tennessee had a rule that to register absentee for your first election, you had to physically go to whatever department and turn in your form in person to get an absentee ballot, and I was at school, so I wasn't able to vote." I was surprised by this story, but after consulting the Tennessee secretary of state's website, I found the following information: "Unless an individual who has registered to vote by mail is on the permanent absentee voting register, that person must appear in person to vote in the first election after the registration becomes effective."[15] In other words, in Tennessee, in order to register to vote absentee for the first time, you must vote in person! Perhaps this rule was not designed to suppress the student vote, but it is an effective way to do it.

Students are among those groups most subject to voter suppression, yet one rarely hears the subject discussed in these terms. Some states have moved polling places off campus to make voting harder for students. Thirty states have strict voter ID laws that disproportionately harm students, who are less likely to have government-issued IDs that include their school address, and seven states do not accept any form of a student ID as proof of residence.[16]

Many apparently small barriers, only indirectly related to voting, were also perceived as having an impact; figuring out how to vote absentee is complicated, but so is finding the time to get a stamp and walk to the post office. One student said she had friends who seemed to think that a trip to the post office took a big effort. Another suggested, "People assume Harvard students are politically engaged, but many students think, 'Hey, we're Harvard students. We're part of twenty clubs, so voting isn't the highest priority.' The time they spend trying to figure out the absentee system might be better spent on a problem set or something."[17] When one student said that the technical aspects might dissuade some from voting, another answered him immediately, pointing out, "If you can change your mailing address on Amazon Prime, you can take the time to change it with your voter rolls." Stamps came up multiple times in different focus groups. I learned that today's young people don't own stamps, and don't always know where to get them.[18]

The job of the facilitator of a focus group is to ask good questions, listen carefully, and make sure that everyone gets a chance to talk. The facilitator is not supposed to say much and certainly is not supposed to lecture or correct anyone. As a professor who has taught undergraduates for almost thirty years, I found it hard to restrain myself when the students talked about how hard voting is. I wanted to tell them they were among the smartest and most capable young people in our country, and if they could get into Harvard, they could figure out how to vote. But I kept quiet. If some of the smartest and most motivated students in our country feel that voting is too hard and too confusing, I realized, we need some serious forms of networked responsibility to help them. Those who got into Harvard had lots of help from parents, teachers, high school counselors, and tutors, as well as books and websites with titles like "How They Got into Harvard." There is a committed network of people helping every student who gets into Harvard. As of early 2018, at least, it appeared that no comparable networks existed to help students vote. Are we such a prestige-conscious, merit driven, and competitive society that we devote intense energy to college admissions but are not concerned enough about democracy to help young adults figure out voter registration and absentee voting?

Everyone seems to assume that college students, especially Ivy League students, do not need advice or help to vote. When I told my neighbor I was writing this chapter, he said, "Well, you certainly don't have to tell Harvard students how to vote." My husband added his favorite quip, "You can always tell a Harvard man, but you can't tell him much."

These descriptions did not fit the students in my focus groups. Many pointed out the ways in which the U.S. voting system is genuinely complicated and antiquated. "For example, in Virginia, the deadline to apply for an absentee ballot is way before the election, and it's a problem. People I know who are very politically engaged missed the deadline because the idea that you have to do something so simple a month and a half in advance is kind of ridiculous. In some places the systems are so antiquated, it's really hard."[19]

Other students expressed real remorse when their genuine efforts to vote failed. "In my first-ever vote, my first-ever-attempted vote, I forgot to put a stamp on the mail-in ballot, . . . and it was returned to me too late for me to resend it, and I did feel like I had really, really messed up."[20] These students didn't treat voting as a deeply private issue, and they seemed willing to share embarrassing stories.

No one should assume that people know what to do when it comes to voting. Networks of institutions and individuals need to gather together to help one another vote. I taught for many years at the University of Minnesota, and I came to understand that my students often did not know where or how to vote but did not want to ask. So I devoted class time to the mechanics of voting—how to register, where to cast a ballot, and how to handle absentee voting, an especially important and difficult issue for students.

HOW TO CHANGE NORMS AND PRACTICES AROUND VOTING

Another student asked what it would take to change attitudes about voting: "There are definitely things that have become not socially acceptable very quickly . . . especially homophobia, even five to ten years ago, that was in a much different place than it is in now. I think if there was a similar culture around its not being okay to think it's cool to not vote—I think that would be a good place, if we could get there."[21] Students recognize and applaud that certain norms have changed dramatically in a short time, but they do not think norms around voting have changed. Why have norms against homophobia been seen as important while voting remains a personal choice? Perhaps because homophobia is seen as directly, personally hurting people they know, while not voting is not seen as hurting anybody.

One student said, "In the U.S. I don't think politics is serious enough that voting is a life or death matter. . . . In the U.S., the fact that you can ignore politics and be fine for the most part makes us unique and makes not voting not that bad." Immediately, an African American student replied, "I disagree with what you said about its not being a life or death question because for marginalized groups in this country, it *is* a life and death question, based on who's voted into power." Nevertheless, she continued, "People feel like their vote doesn't matter. Regardless of how they vote, the worst is going to happen because it happened over and over and over again. That's why there's such a low voter turnout." The first student tried to clarify his remark: "I do agree that for some people it is actually a matter of life and death or being able to stay in the country or not, but what I mean generally and in most U.S. elections, I think people feel like voting doesn't really impact them personally." The other student responded, "I think it's selfish to vote depending on whether it impacts you personally or not. As a citizen, you need to think of where your country is going and about the people you're living with and how it's going to affect you."[22]

Who takes office—the president, members of Congress, Supreme Court justices, or the winners of state and local elections—has influence over many of the issues students care about. State legislatures make decisions about redistricting and voting registration that can make it difficult for students to vote or can dilute their influence. State legislatures also make laws about marriage equality, gun control, immigration, and other issues. Students certainly know these facts, and yet their very low turnout in the midterm elections suggests that they don't take such information to heart.[23]

Many Harvard students still think of voting as a personal issue. While my focus group participants did not treat their own voting choices as deeply private, they did resist the idea they had an obligation to encourage others to vote. Some sense of the inviolability of privacy led all the members of one group to conclude that they could not accept an obligation to get others to vote. One student said, "I feel like there's nothing else implicit in American democracy that says that an American citizen should in any way encourage others to do anything. . . . Like if they don't want to, then they shouldn't have to do that." Another agreed, saying that urging people to vote "gets too close to moral policing."[24]

At the same time, when asked how students, faculty, and the college itself could enhance voter turnout, the groups had many good ideas. One student said that he had never received any information from the university about how or where to vote, and he definitely would have at least looked into it if two weeks before voting day the college had sent a mass email saying, "In case you wanted to vote, here's how to do it."[25] Some mentioned how one student could help another. "For example, some people sent emails over the lists saying, 'I have stamps; come take some and send your ballot.'"[26]

One concrete suggestion was for the university to make a video like those it offers on drug, alcohol, or sexual abuse. Even a "short video on 'how does voting work' or 'this is how you register if you live out of state.' I'm sure some people wouldn't vote, but other people who are just confused might." Another agreed, "Those kinds of campaigns do make a really big difference . . . even though people make fun of them. 'Cool kids vote.' Yeah."[27]

The findings from the focus groups help us understand some of the difficulties voting activists face on campus. I agree with the student who said it would be good if there were a culture on campus saying it's cool to vote. That would be a good place to be if we could get there. But how? The main thing I learned in these groups and from the literature on voter mobilizations is that lecturing students on their responsibility to vote will not motivate them.[28] Nor will messages emphasizing low voter turnout necessarily encourage more voting. A more positive and dynamic strategy emphasizing the possibility of high voter turnout ("Everybody's Voting and So Should You") and developing a sense of excitement and common purpose by creating new norms and practices around voting is a more promising solution.[29] A campus climate with fun or festive things around the elections—from parties to debate watches to bingo nights—creates a buzz and makes a difference.[30]

When I listened to the students in the focus groups lamenting that voting was not considered a cool thing to do, I could not imagine that less than four months later, Harvard students, supported by the IOP, the Ash Center at the Harvard Kennedy School, and the Harvard administration, and many faculty, were going to gear up a very dynamic campaign in the fall of 2018 that would take Harvard students to a whole new level of awareness and mobilization. We were watching changes in norms and practices happening before our eyes in real time. As we saw in chapter 4 and at the Kennedy School's "Getting to 80 Percent" conference in May 2018, norm campaigns around voting were already well under way on the Harvard campus and around the country, so no one was starting from scratch.[31]

From the beginning of the fall semester, students at Harvard University made a major push to increase knowledge about the upcoming 2018 U.S. midterm elections and to encourage students to vote in these elections. The voting campaign was coordinated by the Harvard Votes Challenge, a new organization dedicated to increasing voting on campus. The Harvard Votes Challenge was a non-partisan, university-wide effort organized by the IOP and the Ash Center for Democratic Governance at HKS, challenging each of Harvard's twelve degree-granting schools to increase voter registration and participation among eligible students on their respective campuses. The campaign had extensive involvement from students, especially in the College and at HKS. Teddy Landis, co-chair of the College Harvard Votes Challenge group, said the following:

WHAT DO THE STUDENTS THINK?

I wanted to help create a culture of voting on campus by making voting an event at which the whole community comes together. With Derek Paulhus, I set up the Harvard Votes Challenge, and we challenged all Harvard students to register to vote and to mobilize around the issue of increasing youth voter participation. While voting is, of course, an instrument to push for policy change, etc., the reason I'm so passionate about this issue is because I think the actual act of voting is important in itself. In our country, so many people have fought and died fighting to get the right to vote, and the fact that people aren't using that right to vote is sad to me. . . . It's about recognizing the power of our voices and using them, regardless of the outcome of elections.[32]

The Harvard Votes Challenge got a shot in the arm when the new president of Harvard, Lawrence Bacow, at the convocation ceremony for incoming first-year students, gave students their "first homework assignment": to register to vote and to cast a ballot. This was followed up later in the semester by a message from Dean Rakesh Khurana's encouraging students to vote and President Bacow's email reminding students to register and to vote.[33] The JFK Junior Forum, a program at the IOP, held six events during the fall semester of 2018 on the topic of voting and the midterm election. This number was a significant increase from that of the presidential election season in 2016, when there was only one event that was tangentially related to voting, and during the fall semester of 2014, when there were no events specifically on voting or on the midterms. While a similar increase in programming on voting was happening on campuses elsewhere, a quick survey of events calendars in some other institutions suggests that the number of events at Harvard may have been at the high end.[34]

Students at the Harvard Kennedy School set up their own branch of the Harvard Votes Challenge. Academic Dean (and democracy scholar) Archon Fung and I agreed to serve as faculty advisers. Our goal was to get 90 percent of eligible HKS students to register to vote, a very ambitious target. This was a measurable goal because we were able to work with Turbo-Vote to track student registration numbers at HKS. To our great surprise, we reached our goal on October 16, largely due to a huge lift by student leaders. Though we don't know if all of the registered students voted, research suggests that registered students are more likely to vote, so we still felt it was worthwhile.

The undergraduates also organized the Harvard-Yale Voting Challenge to see which school could get the most students to pledge to vote in the midterm elections. They didn't measure actual registration but just a pledge to vote. Harold Ekeh, co-founder of Yale Votes, said, "There are research studies that have shown that if you commit to vote—whether it's a paper pledge or an online pledge—and you're reminded of it about two weeks before the election, then you're more likely to actually go out and vote." He said his organization's goal was to "change the culture around voting to be more of a celebration of this incredible civic duty."[35] The video the Harvard-Yale Voting Challenge produced together was half the fun. Starting with an old-fashioned film clip of a Yale-Harvard football game, it said, "For 135 years, Harvard and Yale have battled it out on the football field." Then it switched to two young students, one each from Yale and Harvard, who said, "This year, we're battling it out at the ballot box." While the numbers of pledges were not as high as the organizers had hoped, the Harvard-Yale Challenge was just one part of a campaign season of activities.

My research assistant, Roshni Chakraborty, a Harvard College student who did the participant observation research and wrote the memo on which this part of this chapter is based, shared the following personal observations:

> I received 211 emails between August 29 and November 6 about voting in the midterms. The emails encouraged me to register to vote, sent daily reminders about when to cast absentee ballots, sent information on the different systems in different states, and informed me of events related to voting that were taking place on campus. The Harvard Votes Challenge recruited at least one student—called a House Voting Representative—in each undergraduate House to host events in the house related to voting (for example, there was an ice-cream study break where students could also register to vote). I also received 34 personal emails offering to help with absentee ballots, registration, mailing, etc., from friends, proctors, professors, and teaching fellows.[36]

Emily Brother, the house voting representative for Roshni's house, told her, "I definitely think voting is a responsibility. I wish voting was compulsory in our country. Scratch that; I wish we didn't have to make it compulsory and that people voted of their own accord. But till that happens, I wish it was compulsory. I also think that deliberate efforts by political parties to block people from voting are absolutely despicable. Voting should be a lot more accessible. For example, there should be a national holiday to facilitate voting."[37]

A senior who studies with Roshni said that the mood around voting in the fall of 2018 definitely felt different from the mood on campus in 2016: "Voting feels a lot sexier in 2018. It's *the* hot topic on campus right now, and most people seem to recognize that voting is extremely important. I've received countless emails and messages from my friends reminding me to register. On at least six separate occasions, at the end of meetings for clubs and activities, students have asked to make an announcement and reminded everyone which state's absentee ballots are due. There are fliers and posters everywhere that say, 'I will vote on November 6.' You can really feel the change on campus."[38]

The situation on the Harvard campus in the fall of 2018 appeared to be a clear case of the conditions that student voting experts at NSLVE predicted should lead to an increase in voting: "Pervasive political discussions, strong faculty-student relationships coupled with political learning across disciplines, and vibrant electoral activities are attributes of a robust campus climate for political engagement."[39] A group of committed students had organized and worked together with a loose network of administrators, faculty, and staff to take responsibility for helping everyone on campus exercise the right and responsibility to vote.

But what difference did it all make? We know that young people and students voted in record numbers (for midterm elections) in 2018. Exit poll analysis of the Center for Information and Research on Civic Learning and Engagement (CIRCLE) led it to estimate that 31 percent of 18-to-29-year-olds voted in the 2018 midterms, a 50 percent increase from 2014. This level is still well below the youth turnout in presidential elections (46 percent in 2016) but is historically high for midterms. The turnout in 2018 is by far the highest youth participation in the last *seven* midterm elections and the highest midterm youth voter turnout since CIRCLE began doing its analysis in 1994.[40]

But college student voting is not the same as youth voting. We won't have college student voting data and Harvard-specific data until September 2019, when NSLVE finishes and releases its analysis. There are reasons why an increase in Harvard voting might not be as large as the increase in national youth voting. For one thing, by 2016, Harvard was already on the high end of student voting levels due to earlier campaigns (described in chapter 4). For another, Massachusetts did not have the kind of hotly contested elections that were specifically mobilizing the youth vote in places like Wisconsin, Georgia, Nevada, Florida, and Ohio. CIRCLE's data show that the youth vote was particularly strong in states with such contested elections.[41] Even so, I predict an important increase in Harvard voting turnout from the previous midterm, and I would also expect that Harvard numbers will be higher than those of many other comparable institutions in states without hotly contested races.

CHAPTER SIX

Changing Norms and Practices

 NE of the obstacles to increasing voter participation in the United States, as we saw in chapter 5, is the set of ingrained norms and practices about voting in this country. These include the beliefs that we have a right to vote and a right *not* to vote; that there are situations in which not voting is appropriate, even desirable; and that because voting is a private matter, we are being intrusive if we ask people about it or try to encourage them to vote. As we look to the future of voting in this country, we need to think about not only how to get people to the polls, but also how to transform these norms and practices.

If some of the smartest and most motivated young people in our country find voting complicated and difficult, we should assume that many people, especially those who change residences frequently, find it hard to vote. We need networks to assist people in the occasionally difficult practices of registration and voting. Of course, this is a responsibility of the state and of political parties, but we can't leave the task only to them. We know the types of state policies that increase voter turnout: same-day and automatic voter registration; early voting; no-excuse absentee voting and mail-in voting. The problem is that state officials, political party activists, and publics in some places in the United States do not want to expand voter turnout and even actively suppress it. In such situations, networked responsibility of non-state actors to change voting norms and practices is all the more important.

THE NORM WORK TO BE DONE

The work to be done on norms and practices surrounding voting is something for which all of us connected to the problem of non-voting have forward-looking responsibility. This is a true social connection situation, of the kind described by Iris Marion Young, in which all of us have responsibilities. States have responsibilities to enact effective policies for increasing participation. Universities have responsibilities to help their students and staff register by holding events on campus that provide information and assistance for voting in the state or absentee. Professors—especially political science professors but others as well—have a professional and civic responsibility to help students understand how to vote and why they should. Finally, young people have responsibilities to vote, to encourage their friends and acquaintances to vote, and to help create climates on campuses where voting is seen as appropriate. As we saw in chapters 4 and 5, students themselves are already taking the lead on these issues.

Norms are "intersubjective"—that is, norms exist only when they are shared by large groups of people.[1] Thus the process of norm change is complicated. If we have an existing norm—for example, the norm that we have in the United States that there is a right not to vote—how does an old norm get changed to a new one? Norm entrepreneurs start by converting individuals and groups one by one until a cascade-like process that characterizes some norm change can take over. Early anti-smoking activists had to convince individual smokers that smoking was dangerous to their health and the health of others around them until a strong norm against smoking started to emerge. Individuals hold beliefs that political psychologists call "cognitive schemas," or structures used to organize knowledge and memory.[2] At the start of norm change, enough individual schemas have to start changing to add up to norm change. This is always a slow and uncertain process. Sometimes it never happens or gets reversed. There is nothing inevitable about norm change. Some argue that since campaigns to stop smoking or to use seat belts were also about self-interest, such norms should be expected to change more easily and permanently than other norms, like voting, that don't involve self-interest.[3] But we also know that self-interest itself, just like national interest, is a constructed category that may be less obvious than some assume.[4] For women, for example, it would appear to be in their interest to vote, and yet for over half a century, suffragists had a very hard time convincing other women that this was the case. When I refer to "norm work," I thus mean the work of norm entrepreneurs changing individual schemas that, when aggregated, could potentially lead to norm cascades.

Norm Work #1: Voting Is Not Just a Question of Self-Interest and Rationality

One of the comments from the focus group that most stuck in my mind was the following:

> Ideally, I would say of course we should encourage everyone to vote; it's important; it's the heart of democracy. But I don't fully believe it when I say those things. I don't know. I think voting is important, but it's hard for me to talk to people and encourage them to vote when they can come back with pretty good arguments about why their votes don't count and I don't have anything very convincing to say against that.[5]

Why does this student feel this way?

Of those who have some responsibility to construct new norms and practices around voting, I would first like to address my colleagues, professional political scientists. I was struck by how seldom the focus group participants mentioned their professors as people who had encouraged them to vote or helped them understand how to do it. Often, I hear about the opposite: professors who disregard or discourage voting. Some political scientists and economists working from a rational choice perspective have spent many years establishing and propagating the idea that voting is irrational.[6] They argue that the cost of voting—the time and energy it takes—far exceeds its rational benefits—that is, the possibility that their vote will be pivotal in deciding an election. This argument contributes to many students' belief that voting is ineffective and meaningless and therefore irrational. A political scientist I know who does not vote assigns a text on the irrationality of voting in every class he teaches on American politics. The "fact" of voting's irrationality is debatable, depending on the model of rationality, self-interest, and causality one uses, but the focus groups make clear this argument's impact on student voting patterns.[7]

But voting is often motivated by something other than self-interest. Many individuals vote because they believe in democracy and feel a responsibility to vote. Voting, moreover, is social as well as political. It is a way to participate not only in a system of governance, but also in a community. The most persuasive new voting research draws our attention to voting within sociocultural and historical contexts rather than seeing voters as "atomized actors floating unanchored in a homogenized stream of national mass-media stimuli, their perceptions unfiltered by constraining and validating personal relationships."[8] In their book *Mobilizing Inclusion*, Lisa Garcia Bedolla and Melissa Michelson argue that get-out-the-vote conversations with canvassers, for example, can help individuals make changes in their sense of civic identity as voters.

A colleague from the Harvard Kennedy School, Stephen Walt, told me a story about a local election. His wife, Rebecca Stone, is a town meeting member and a school committee member from Brookline, Massachusetts, who is deeply involved in local politics. In one local election, Stone gave Walt clear information about her top candidates for the school committee in a very contested election. That evening, Walt arrived home from work at 6:30 without having voted. Stone asked him if he had voted, and when he said he had forgotten, she urged him to hustle over to the polls, which fortunately didn't close until 8 p.m. The next day they learned that one of Stone's preferred candidates had won the election by one vote—as Walt saw it, his vote.

This story illustrates that voting is not always irrational, even in the narrow economic sense. The idea of the irrational voter is often about national elections, not local ones, where voter turnout is often low and a handful of votes can change the result. But more important, the story shows how voting takes place within the contexts of communities and is not mainly about self-interest but about relationships and identities. This is why the student-led campaigns like those at Harvard University in the fall of 2018 were so important: they were changing the way communities of students thought about themselves and about voting. They increasingly thought of voting as something that was important, even "sexy," and they thought of themselves as having an identity as voters within a community of voters.

Another political science friend told me a story that made me think differently about the irrationality of voting. He and his wife (also a political scientist) went to vote in the 2008 Democratic primary. They did so out of pure obligation since instrumentally voting was irrational: the only election on the ballot in their state was for the presidential nomination, and they favored different candidates, so their votes would cancel one another out. When they got to the polls, they were told they could not vote because the records showed they had voted in the Republican primary in the previous election. This was a mistake. They protested and were promised that the voting station would look into it and that they should come back in the late afternoon. When they returned, they discovered that their local voting board had discovered a major human error that had threatened to disenfranchise scores of voters.

At a minimum, all professors who teach about the "irrationality" of voting should also teach about the surprising difference between actual voter turnout and the irrationality hypothesis, engaging students in a discussion of why so many people, contrary to what economists would predict, turn out to vote. Then they should teach the latest literature on voter mobilization, showing how interactive canvassing can change the self-perceptions and behavior of citizens. While they are at it, they should provide information about the logistics of voting, thus decreasing the cost of voting for their students.

Norm Work #2: There Is Not a Right Not to Vote

Virtually all the students in the Harvard focus groups, even those who felt strongly that they had a responsibility to vote, believed they had a right *not* to vote. Obviously, they have a *choice* not to vote, an action for which they will not be sanctioned and that carries little social stigma, but I asked a different question: Do you believe you have a *right* not to vote? In this country, many believe we have both a right to vote and a right not to vote, but we often do not speak about a responsibility to vote. My conversations with Harvard students persuaded me that the belief in the right not to vote is even more prevalent than I had imagined.

After my second Castle Lecture at Yale, in which I talked about the responsibility to vote and I mentioned that Americans believe they have a right not to vote, I got vigorous pushback from my friend and colleague Harold Koh, former dean of Yale Law School. Koh argued that we do not have a right not to vote any more than we have a right not to perform other duties of citizenship—paying taxes or serving on a jury, for example.[9] After thinking about this, I decided that it is indeed a norms issue. Whether or not this right exists legally is less important than its existence as a shared understanding about appropriate behavior. As a norm, it influences all of our practices surrounding voting. It would be useful to change the norm so that we recognize both a right and a responsibility to vote. Although people would still be able to choose not to vote, that choice would not be graced with the language of rights. Such a norm would also make voter suppression more difficult since it would be seen as preventing people from exercising a positive responsibility.[10]

A right is something to which one is morally or legally entitled. Asserting a right not to vote thus indicates a special entitlement not to vote. The rights of U.S. citizens are recognized in the Constitution and its Bill of Rights and in various international human rights declarations and treaties. None of these documents acknowledges a right not to vote. The U.S. Constitution, which mentions the right to vote five times, more than any other right, makes no mention of a right *not* to vote; nor has the Supreme Court ever defined such a right.[11] Jury duty is mandatory, and, in some states, missing jury duty can lead to a prison sentence or a fine of up to one thousand dollars. As we know too well, failing to pay taxes can lead to fines or criminal prosecution, and failing to register for or comply with the Military Selective Service Act is punishable by a large fine or prison term or both. Voting is different in the sense that no coercion or constraint will oblige one to go to the polls. Such lack of constraint is different, however, from having a right—that is, a moral and legal entitlement not to vote.

Inspired by Koh, I asked one of my focus groups, after students told me they had a right not to vote, whether they had a right not to pay taxes, not to do jury duty, or not to register for Selective Service. They recognized that there was no right not to carry out those civic duties. If taxes, jury duty, military service, and voting are four of the core duties of citizenship, why would only one of them carry a corresponding right not to perform it? The others are far more onerous, time consuming, and, in the case of military service, even dangerous. Why would the lightest of our civic duties alone carry a right not to perform it? Of course, we want the responsibility of participation in our political life to reach far beyond voting, but it starts there and is a necessary piece of our responsibilities.

Norm Work #3: Claim a Role for Agency

In discussing rights and individual responsibilities, including especially the responsibility to vote, we revive a debate about structure and agency. For social scientists, agency implies the possibility that individuals and groups can act independently and make their own free choices. Agency is not the ability to assert power or control but the possibility of intention and the freedom of subjectivity.[12] There is a longstanding belief in the social sciences that stressing individual responsibility and agency in the face of systemic and structural factors is naïve at best and pernicious at worst. In this view, too much attention to individual responsibility distracts us from the "real" structural causes of injustice and from the responsibility of the state, political parties, and our economic system for our predicament.

As a political scientist, I understand the economic and political barriers to voting in this country. Single-member districts and a winner-take-all system lead to two political parties struggling to attract the swing votes at the center. Gerrymandering, voter suppression, and the power of dark money in our political system shape the candidates and issues brought before the public and make people disenchanted with the system.[13] The Electoral College makes whole chunks of the country feel essentially written off in presidential elections, so people do not vote because they believe their votes will not count. Smaller institutional features also make a difference. We vote on Tuesdays and Election Day is not a holiday, so working people find it hard to vote. We live in a very mobile country, and yet our voter registration system is geared to a past when people rarely moved. Nothing I say about the responsibility to vote means we should ignore the systemic or structural factors that lead to low voter turnout.

I take from Arendt the idea that even where structures are powerful and determine outcomes, personal action is possible and necessary and cannot be "practically useless," at least in the long term. Arendt argues that we cannot retreat from responsibility by stressing structural causality. Near the end of *Eichmann in Jerusalem*, she refers directly to the theories that may serve as reasons to dismiss individual responsibility. "Another such escape from the area of ascertainable facts and personal responsibility," she writes, "are the countless theories, based on non-specific, abstract, hypothetical assumptions—from the Zeitgeist down to the Oedipus complex—which are all so general that they explain and justify every event and every deed; no alternative to what actually happened is even considered and

no person could have acted differently from the way he did act.
. . . All these clichés have in common that they make judgment
superfluous and that to utter them is devoid of all risk."[14]

Like Arendt, I believe we must be careful not to let theory
justify inaction or to imply that there is no possible alternative
to what actually happened. Regardless of structural con-
straints, we each have to make judgments—about what is
right and wrong, as well as what works and does not work.
Understanding the structural barriers to voting does not
mean that individual agency is impossible or irrelevant.

Norm Work #4: Talk about a Politics and an Ethic of Responsibility

One political science colleague told me that the structures of capitalism and the influence of money in the U.S.
political system were so powerful that voting was not only
useless, but also perhaps pernicious because it legitimized an
illegitimate system. A few students in the Harvard focus
groups took a similar position. They remind me of arguments
made by the left in Latin America as the region careened toward authoritarianism in the 1970s. One might respond with
Weber's ethic of responsibility: in addition to a responsibility
to act, we have a responsibility to think about the effects of
our actions. An ethic of responsibility is not only about individual efficacy, but also about collective efficacy. When a student or colleague tells me that she actively does not vote as a
symbolic protest against the problems of our electoral system,
I do not doubt the sincerity of her intentions, but I do question whether this is responsible in the best sense—whether
she is taking into account the consequences of her actions.

What impact do people who refuse to vote as a protest against an unjust system actually have? We cannot know because their non-votes are not recorded. There is no way to determine what percentage of U.S. voters do not vote as a matter of protest or face voter suppression or are simply indifferent or lazy.

If we had voting machines like the ones used in Brazil, people could register their protest vote. In Brazil, where voting is compulsory, the voting machines have two buttons to let you protest—one button says you refuse to vote, and the other says you vote in blank. In other words, if one is going to refuse to vote in protest, it must be just as hard as voting. There is no easy option that lets one both feel self-righteous and not have to work very hard at it. Within such a system, a protest vote could potentially affect politics. I do not think compulsory voting would work in the United States since we have such a strong belief in our right not to vote, but Brazil's system, unlike ours, makes a protest vote intelligible and potentially effective.

In the United States, some apparent protest non-votes by disenchanted voters on the left may have swayed the 2016 elections. For example, in the key swing states of Michigan, Wisconsin, and Pennsylvania, many voters who had supported Barack Obama in 2012 failed to go to the polls in November 2016 or gave their votes to third-party candidates. The cumulative effect of those decisions was that Donald Trump carried each of these states by less than 1 percentage point and won the presidency. Someone motivated by what Weber called a pure "ethic of intention" might feel that he had exercised his responsibility by refraining from voting because he wished to protest the limited choices the political system made available, regardless of the consequences of that decision. In Weber's ethic of responsibility, however, both voters and non-voters bear responsibility for the outcome of elections.

Norm Work #5: Encouraging Others to Vote

We need new norms, not only about an individual's responsibility to vote, but also about a collective responsibility to encourage and help others to vote. Much of the voting literature tells us that the key to motivating citizens to vote is personal partisan mobilization. "Partisan" suggests that citizens are primarily motivated by their feelings for or against the parties in office, but it would be a mistake to forget that the most effective methods are also personal.[15] Political parties can use personal contact methods (door-to-door canvassing, phone calls) to encourage or remind individuals to vote; such methods have been found to be more effective than impersonal methods such as texts, physical mail, email, or social media.[16] For greatest effectiveness, however, the encouragement must also be "personal" in another sense: "People are most motivated to act when contacted by people whom they know."[17] People are more likely to vote when encouraged by their family and friends. We also know that peer pressure can be persuasive. To be able to encourage others to vote, we need to overcome the idea that voting is such a private affair that we should not even ask others whether they are voting, much less urge them to do so.

The students in my focus groups are not the only ones who hesitate to encourage others to vote. I discussed the issue with my colleague Alexander Keyssar, who has written an important book on the history of the right to vote in this country.[18] He explained that many people need to "overcome discomfort" in order to encourage their friends and acquaintances to vote. When I asked why, he said that people think it is the job of political parties and campaigns to get out the vote and not a responsibility of individuals or other organizations such as universities.

As we know, however, it is in the interest of some parties, some campaigns, and some candidates to suppress votes. We cannot leave it to opposition parties and campaigns alone to do the work of getting out the vote. We need to enlist the power of peer pressure and normative change to increase voter turnout.

IS THIS POSSIBLE?

You may be thinking that it will be difficult or impossible to make the changes described above, but I have seen and studied major norm shifts in my lifetime. For example, the recycling rate in the United States has more than tripled over the last thirty years, reaching a point in 2015 where 34 percent of municipal solid waste was recycled or composted.[19] This has happened without a national law mandating recycling but through a variety of state, community, and individual initiatives. Dramatic changes in norms and practices are very possible. Most people spend much more time and energy recycling than they do voting, even though voting is more likely to affect the environment than is recycling. Archon Fung points out that universities spend vastly more time encouraging students, staff, and faculty to recycle and compost than encouraging them to vote. What would it be like, he asks us, to have universities make a similar commitment to thinking about how we can make democracy better?[20]

Among the young, watching my sons and comparing their experiences to my own at their age, I see how some norms and practices have changed dramatically—for example, those around drunk driving and the idea of the designated driver. Young people seem to drink as much as their parents did at that age, but they are not driving drunk as much. Today, someone takes the responsibility of being the designated driver, and then someone else does it the next time. The norm has changed through a mix of government initiatives, civil society activism, and peer pressure so that it has become appropriate, indeed expected, for someone to volunteer to be the designated driver. Drunk driving remains a life-and-death issue, but such dramatic changes in youth behavior show that ingrained norms and practices can change.

The dynamism I witnessed at Harvard around voting in the fall of 2018, the new "democracy movement" described by authors like Lappe and Eichen, and the campaigns around the country that participants in the Getting to 80% Conference shared give me some confidence that we may be witnessing significant changes in youth voting behavior in the United States that could have a lasting impact on our political system.

CHAPTER SEVEN

The Rights and Responsibilities Framework
on Campus: Speech and Sexual Assault

Y book *Evidence for Hope* defends human rights law, institutions, and movements against what I thought were unsubstantiated critiques.[1] In this book, however, I have elaborated my own critique and my recommendations for ways to implement human rights more effectively by embracing responsibilities. This is not a book about responsibilities *rather than* rights or about the responsibilities of non-state actors *rather than* those of states. It is about the necessity of creating and articulating firmer norms and practices of networked responsibilities among diverse actors as necessary complements to human rights in order to realize those rights more fully.

The rights-and-responsibility theme is a useful frame for analyzing many issues. By itself, the human rights approach is excessively state-centric, often directing our attention to state and (increasingly) corporate responsibility but not to the political responsibilities of all the possible agents of justice. This rights-and-responsibility frame has been a fruitful way to think about the silences in debates over some rights—such as digital privacy—that come from our thinking about rights being too state-centric. My framework doesn't yield a list of specific responsibilities for different actors, but it is a useful way of thinking about problems. The practice of networked responsibility for human rights is everywhere around us, but the norms and discourses of non-state responsibility are often absent, as is an explicit framework for strategizing about responsibility.

The rights-and-responsibility framework requires us to ask the following questions:

(1) What are the relevant rights in question? The framework always starts with rights but acknowledges that these are not enough—not because there is something inherently lacking in rights but because identifying the rights issue at stake is only the first step toward the realization of rights. We must also assign and assume responsibilities to implement rights.

(2) Who are the relevant agents of justice who are socially connected to the rights violation and able to take action? Very often, states are the first and most important agents to whom we assign responsibility. In some cases, corporations also have responsibility. But we usually cannot stop there. This step also implies a more complete brainstorming

to identify relevant agents socially connected to a rights violation who could take action to remedy it. In addition to states and corporations, these agents might include international organizations; non-governmental organizations; social movements; local governments; professional associations; institutions; individuals; and an important group, the victims of human rights violations.

(3) Ask what together we can do. What types of forward-looking political and ethical responsibilities could be exercised by these multiple agents of justice? In many cases, particular forms of exercising responsibility may be discretionary so that each part of a network may take on a small part of the effort, knowing that others are doing their share.

(4) Good intentions are not enough. We also need an ethic of responsibility that directs us to be conscious of the impacts of our actions. Using the best tools at our disposal, how can we choose actions that are most likely to be effective?

These questions reflect what human rights movements have often tried to do in practice. In rhetoric, they assigned responsibility primarily to states and stressed responsibility as liability; in practice, they often *assumed* responsibility and worked in networks with other agents of justice to bring about change. In this chapter, I will use two short cases to illustrate how things might change if we explicitly adopted a rights-and-responsibility frame to approach key issues on campus like the right to protest and the right to be free from sexual assault.

I chose these cases because they help deepen our thinking about a series of important and controversial rights and responsibility issues. First, both cases make clear that focusing on state responsibility alone, and on backward-looking responsibility as liability, are completely inadequate ways to address many human rights issues. To more fully implement rights, we must also focus on the forward-looking responsibility of diverse non-state actors. Second, these cases show that for non-state actors to assume responsibility for rights is not at all simple because a given rights scenario may create multiple and even conflicting responsibilities. Finally, the cases can deepen our understanding of how Max Weber's "ethic of responsibility" relates to the overall argument.[2] It is not enough for non-state actors to assume complex responsibilities with the intention of promoting human rights. We must also think about the consequences of our actions.

Iris Young explains that because her social connection model is open and discretionary, it cannot provide rules or a method for calculating what to do. She says non-state socially connected agents cannot be blamed for contributing to injustice or be found at fault when they try to rectify injustice but do not succeed. They can, however, be criticized "for not taking action, not taking enough action, taking ineffective action, or taking action that is counterproductive."[3] This important distinction between blaming and criticizing has been lost in the debate over responsibility and needs to be reclaimed. I would go one step further and suggest that we have even lost the distinction among blaming, criticizing, and proposing action. In a forward-looking responsibility model that takes effectiveness into account, we need to be able to criticize ineffective action as well as propose policies that could be more effective. To be unable to do so is to leave our critical facilities at the door. Weber's ethic of responsibility tells us that we also need to engage our best knowledge about what is effective or not effective.

RIGHTS AND RESPONSIBILITIES FOR SPEECH AND PROTEST

During my Castle Lectures, various members of the audience pointed out that they believe the Trump administration has ushered in a dangerous time for our country and that citizens have a series of responsibilities to protect their democracy.

These are also perilous times on some campuses. In North Carolina, a researcher reported that anti-Semitic stickers and Nazi symbols were placed around one campus; at another, white supremacists hoisted banners with slogans about their group, Identity Evropa, in the center of campus to "welcome" new students.[4] When someone at the University of North Carolina–Greensboro chalked sidewalks with the words "Deport Them," it was the student who washed the words away who was brought up on disciplinary charges. Meanwhile, the North Carolina legislature passed a law forbidding students at the civil rights clinics at their law schools from participating in litigation, even though the main purpose of clinical programs is to prepare students for practical work in the law, including, of course, litigation.[5]

It is essential to protect our institutions in exceptional times.[6] Much of the point of chapters 4–6 above is the idea that one key way we can protect our democracy is by voting and helping others to vote. But how do we protect our institutions while also protecting the rights to free speech and protest at our universities? Do we need exceptional criteria for exceptional times? If so, what are they?

Using the rights-and-responsibilities framework, we realize that the right at stake is the right to speech, including the right to protest. These rights are not only essential in and of themselves; they are also crucial tools for advancing and protecting other rights. We need the right to speech and protest, for example, to advance other civil, political, economic, and social rights.[7]

The state is of course a key agent in the protection of speech and protest, but state action alone is completely inadequate for forward-looking responsibility. The U.S. Supreme Court's definition of free speech is a starting place but not at all sufficient for the complex speech issues we face on campuses. Supreme Court rulings are about responsibility as liability: what limits of speech we must obey in order not to get arrested, sued, or imprisoned. It is important and useful to know, for example—as many college students do not—that we do *not* have a right in this country not to be confronted with hurtful speech. In a survey of fifteen hundred students at colleges around the country, 44 percent said that the First Amendment does not protect hate speech, compared to 39 percent who said it does and 16 percent who didn't know.[8] As interpreted by the U.S. Supreme Court, the free-speech protections in the First Amendment are so broad that they admit only a handful of exceptions, such as speech that is likely to incite immediate unlawful action, that constitutes a "true threat," or, in some cases, that is obscene.[9] In other words, much of what we call "hate speech" is indeed protected by the First Amendment.

Many college students in the 1960s and 1970s grew up approving of these free-speech protections as enabling protests against the Vietnam War and other U.S. government policies.[10] But on campus today, many do not see free speech as helping them protest. Instead they associate it "with bullying and shame."[11]

Supreme Court doctrine is only a starting place, and using it alone would be inappropriate for many of the speech issues we face on campus. We are interested also in forward-looking responsibilities for speech and protest that will help us fashion a world where the enjoyment of multiple rights is ever more possible. Universities, faculty, and students all have responsibilities in this context, and since they are the proximate actors connected to campus free-speech issues, they have the strongest obligation to exercise these responsibilities.

At the same time, our responsibilities are complex. They are completely different if we're engaged in a protest on the street, in the audience of a panel, or in charge of a discussion in a classroom.[12] On the street, I'm free to shout down others but not in the audience at a panel. My colleague Archon Fung explained why a Supreme Court "free-speech absolutist view" is often inappropriate for thinking about speech in classrooms and campuses. If he addressed a white student in his class as "redneck" or if a student called him "Chink Professor," they would be protected under the First Amendment. But such language would be "completely inconsistent with pedagogical and collegial obligations," and Fung could "expect a call from my department head or dean to ask me to refrain from such conduct."[13] Fung in turn would be expected to talk to the student about classroom norms. Should the student persist in such behavior, he could be asked to leave the course.

Not only do we have different responsibilities in different settings, but we also have potentially conflicting responsibilities in the same setting. My colleague Dani Rodrik spelled some of these out in a thought-provoking column entitled "How Should Universities Handle the Trump Administration?" He argued that because the Trump administration is an "odious presidency" and Trump himself "violates on a daily basis the norms on which liberal democracy rests," those who serve him, whatever their role, are tainted by his acts. This means that academic institutions need to "tread a narrow path" of making sure people can hear and speak diverse viewpoints, including those of the Trump administration, but they must not do anything that would appear to normalize and legitimate such a presidency.[14] How to do this is complicated, but Rodrik recommends that universities should do nothing to honor Trump officials: "no honorific titles (fellow, senior fellow), no named lecture, no keynote speeches." Invitations to Trump officials, he writes, should never come from senior university authorities, nor should such authorities grace the presentations of such officials. All events should feature opportunities for "vigorous questioning and debate."[15]

I understand that sometimes we feel we have not only a right but also a responsibility to protest the odious nature of some arguments and practices. Torture is my push-button issue, for example, and I joined a protest against John Yoo, one of the authors of the Bush administration's "torture memos," at the American Political Science Association's annual meeting in 2017. Our protest involved silently turning our backs on Yoo and holding up signs, not shouting him down.[16]

But universities, as places of free inquiry, have an absolute obligation to present diverse viewpoints, encourage the free speech of all students and faculty, avoid both formal and informal censorship, and engage with the leaders of the day.[17] When they get this balance wrong, they harm the educational experience in this country. For example, in the spring of 2017, some conservative students at Middlebury College invited Charles Murray of the American Enterprise Institute to speak on campus. Other students and some faculty opposed Murray because they saw him as an anti-gay white nationalist. Some considered his 1994 book, *The Bell Curve*, a work of racism couched in the language of research.[18]

The conservative students asked political science professor Allison Stanger to moderate the panel, and she agreed. Even though Stanger is a Democrat and disagrees with Murray on many issues, she believed the students had a right to invite a speaker of their choice to campus. As the event got under way, Murray was drowned out by chants of "What is the enemy? White supremacy!" and "Racist, sexist, anti-gay: Charles Murray, go away." Because it was impossible to hear Murray speak, he, Stanger, and the event organizers went to another site and broadcasted the discussion via live stream. When Murray left with Stanger and Middlebury's vice president for communications, a mob charged them, pulling Stanger's hair and shoving her. Stanger spent weeks recovering from a concussion and wearing a neck brace for whiplash. After the encounter she wrote a critique of the protesters in an op-ed piece in the *New York Times:*

For us to engage with one another as fellow human beings—even on issues where we passionately disagree—we need reason, not just emotions. Middlebury students could have learned from identifying flawed assumptions or logical shortcomings in Dr. Murray's arguments. They could have challenged him in the Q. and A. If the ways in which his misinterpreted ideas have been weaponized precluded hearing him out, students also had the option of protesting outside, walking out of the talk or simply refusing to attend.[19]

Charles Murray also came to Harvard in the fall of 2017 for a talk, and students protested in a different way. There were protestors outside the hall where the event was taking place, and there were protestors inside as well who held up banners and signs halfway through his talk and then walked out. Charles Murray responded to this approach during the talk and said, "This is way better than Middlebury. I appreciate the way that was done." After the talk, some faculty members held a discussion on Murray's work and his talk.[20]

At the Harvard Kennedy School in the fall of 2017, we faced our own test of the rights and responsibilities of speech and protest on campus when Betsy DeVos, secretary of education, was invited to speak about school choice. It was the first visit of a Trump administration cabinet member to Harvard, and it came right after a student group planning a "Free-Speech Week" at Berkeley had cancelled the event. Archon Fung, then the academic dean at the Kennedy School and a scholar of deliberative democracy, opened the event with some ground rules:

> In this time of deep division, what we need most is to listen and to understand one another instead of circling the wagons into our own separate echo chambers. The Kennedy School is

all about understanding differences and building bridges. But creating inclusive space is especially difficult these days because many people from all sides would rather shut the other down rather than hear what they are saying. . . . Shutting people down is contrary to the values of this space and of the Harvard Kennedy School. Here, we encourage the exchange of ideas and different viewpoints. Even if we do not agree, it is important to hear, and allow others in attendance to listen and speak as well.[21]

Fung went on to say that he would ask the university police to escort from the forum anyone who insisted on preventing others from speaking or hearing by disrupting the event. Members of the public went through a search as they entered the forum, and some protest signs were confiscated. When some signs were nonetheless hung from the railing of some upper balconies, Dean Fung decided they were not disrupting anyone's speech and that the event would go on. DeVos's talk proceeded without disruptions, and the questions and debates were challenging and tense.

Rodrik and Fung have different approaches to finding the correct balance between our rights and responsibilities to speech and protest on campus. Rodrik might have argued that Fung shouldn't have introduced DeVos's presentation because he was academic dean and his presence legitimated the odious Trump presidency. But I think Rodrik may underestimate the role institutional leaders have in making sure universities are open to diverse viewpoints. In the case of DeVos's speech, we needed Fung to make sure DeVos would be heard; his authority, not only as a dean but also as a progressive scholar of deliberative democracy, helped ensure that DeVos could speak.

This issue also obliges us to turn to the question of an ethic of responsibility and the effects of our actions. Many students believe they have a responsibility not only to defend institutions, but also to defend fellow students in particular, and oppressed people more generally, against hurtful and degrading speech. The 2017 national survey of fifteen hundred undergraduate students shows that 51 percent of them agree that it is acceptable for student groups to disrupt a speaker who is making "offensive and hurtful statements" by loudly and repeatedly shouting so the audience cannot hear. Nineteen percent of students agree that it is acceptable for student groups to use violence to prevent a speaker from speaking.[22] These undergraduates feel a deep sense of responsibility to protect vulnerable groups from hurtful, offensive, or biased speech.[23] Their view is not "no responsibility" but *different* responsibility.

Although I understand these students' positive intentions, violence and drowning out the speech of others is problematic from the point of view of the ethic of responsibility. Presumably we do not protest only for expressive reasons, but also because we want to make a difference or change something. In other words, we want an effective protest. In order to be effective, we need to think hard about our tactics because these tactics and the responses to them can help us persuade others, or they can turn others against us. In the struggle over free speech, in addition to our ethical responsibility not to silence the speech of others, it is smart to consider not just what is right to do, but also what works.

In this country, the use of violent tactics virtually always alienates exactly the constituencies groups must attract in order to win broader support for their ideas. For example, at Middlebury, the people protesting hate speech can't afford to lose the support of the Allison Stangers on campus—that is, respected senior figures who are generally in sympathy with their political views or are at least ready to be sympathetic. Social scientists have shown that in addition to the political fallout that violent campaigns create, such campaigns are usually less effective than nonviolent campaigns. For example, in their book *Why Civil Resistance Works: The Strategic Logic of Nonviolent Conflict*, Erica Chenoweth and Maria Stephan show that between 1900 and 2006, campaigns of nonviolent resistance were more than twice as effective as their violent counterparts. They attribute this success mainly to the nonviolent campaigns' greater ability to attract widespread popular support, which helps separate regimes from their main sources of power.[24] Whether or not you agree with my argument about the responsibility to not block the speech of others, if you want to be effective, you will find that you persuade more people if you act nonviolently.

SEXUAL ASSAULT ON CAMPUS

The issue of sexual assault on campus requires us once again to think about the importance of multiple agents of justice. "Sexual assault" is a large umbrella category that includes any non-consensual sexual activity or contact, including but not limited to rape. As with all the issues I have discussed here, I believe that everyone socially connected to this injustice bears some responsibility for the solution, including the people who have suffered harm.

This issue also points us again to the need for forward-looking responsibility in addition to backward-looking responsibility. The debate over sexual assault on campus is almost completely framed in terms of liability or blame. Such backward-looking responsibility is absolutely essential for justice and for the psychological and physical well-being of many victims. But we also need to think about the forward-looking responsibility of multiple agents of justice, especially how potential victims, as capable agents, can take measures to prevent future violence. Some victims prefer to be called survivors, and others prefer neither term. The Office of Sexual Assault Prevention and Response (OSAPR) on the Harvard campus uses the term "survivor" or simply "people who have experienced harm."[25]

My interest in treating survivors as capable agents is more than academic. When I was eighteen years old, I spent the summer in Mexico studying Spanish at a university program in Guadalajara. I lived in the home of a Mexican family and shared a room with another U.S. student, Holly. One night, Holly invited me out on the town with her new Mexican boyfriend, whom I did not know well. I drank way too many margaritas. At one point, Holly's boyfriend asked me to leave with him and took me to a room where we had sex. At the time, I didn't think of it as sexual assault; that word was not even part of my vocabulary. I hadn't protested, and I had felt almost drugged and that I was sleepwalking through the events. I may have believed that I inadvertently consented by not resisting. Now I do consider it a sexual assault because I understand that there are certain situations where consent is not possible. Although I did not resist, the sexual contact was unwelcome to me, and I have recalled it as such my entire life. Even so, I didn't tell many people, including my family when I returned home. I didn't talk to Holly about it, and I never saw her boyfriend again.

I decided I had to help myself. Partly consciously, but mainly unconsciously, I decided that I would try never to be caught in that situation again. Was I blaming myself? I didn't feel as if I was. I was just learning from the experience and determined not to let it happen again. From that time, I have never been drunk in a public setting or a private setting with unfamiliar people. I developed a keener eye for trouble, I think, by identifying the kinds of situations and people that are likely to be trouble and have consistently tried to avoid them by drinking less, not going certain places at certain times, and following my instincts.

When preparing this text, I read a line in an article that seems in retrospect to capture what I might have said about this incident when it happened if I had been able to articulate it. "While rape is always only the perpetrator's fault—and I mean *always*—being smart about your risk shouldn't be controversial."[26] Let me repeat and develop this thought so that I am not misunderstood. Any effort to limit sexual assault must first hold perpetrators responsible—and, where appropriate, criminally accountable. Training to prevent future sexual assault must first focus on potential perpetrators, including the setting out of clear rules for what constitutes consent and the conditions under which no consent is possible. Bystander training is also important. What was my roommate doing at the time? I can't remember, but I needed her help and didn't get it.

Bystander training is one type of a forward-looking prevention strategy for campus sexual assault. A bystander intervention describes a situation where someone who isn't directly involved steps in to change the outcome. The purpose of bystander training is to convert a passive bystander into an active bystander or into what some people are now calling "upstanders," or "people who intervene to help others in need."[27] OSAPR explains bystander training as follows, using the language of responsibility: "Research has found that people struggle with whether helping out is their responsibility—a concept referred to as diffusion of responsibility. . . . Successful bystander intervention programs teach people to overcome their resistance to checking in and helping out. They raise an individual's self efficacy—or, confidence in one's ability to perform the necessary action."[28] Bystander training is relevant not only to campus sexual assault, but also to other forms of harassment. For example, Hollaback, a movement to end street harassment powered by a network of local activists, offers bystander intervention webinars to help people learn how to speak up and intervene effectively when they see harassment happening.[29]

Even as we recognize that sexual assault is always the perpetrator's fault, we need to focus on risk reduction for victims. That also involves training women to recognize potentially dangerous situations and have strategies to avoid them. We want to condemn and protest sexual assault and also make sure we adopt effective policies so that fewer and fewer people experience it.

Using the rights-and-responsibilities framework, we can identify the relevant rights (to be free from campus sexual assault) and assign responsibilities to very diverse institutions, groups, and individuals, including but not limited to the university administration, students, faculty, staff, fraternities, bystanders, sports teams and their coaches, and victims or survivors themselves. A number of state laws and policies have proven to be effective deterrents to violence against women more generally. For example, one of the best legal remedies available to domestic violence victims is the use of a civil order for protection, which requires violent offenders to leave the home.[30] More recent laws requiring bystander reporting and intervention are another promising development.[31]

We have little information about what works to prevent sexual assault on campus. When we come to the final step—thinking about what works—we may be stymied. We don't know nearly as much as we would like about how to prevent sexual assault on campus.

First, we should start with what we know about its prevalence. Much of the data I use here refers to sexual assault against women, but we know that men and transgender college students also experience sexual assault. Sexual assault against transgender students, in fact, is especially high. Twenty-one percent of TGQN (transgender, genderqueer, nonconforming) college students have been sexually assaulted, compared to 18 percent of non-TGQN women and 4 percent of non-TGQN men.[32] Undergraduate students are between two to three times more likely to be victims of sexual abuse than graduate students. According to a survey by the Association of American Universities (AAU), "Among undergraduate students, 23.1% of females and 5.4% of males experience rape or sexual assault through physical force, violence, or incapacitation."[33] Freshmen experience more sexual assault than upperclassmen, and more than 50 percent of college sexual assaults occur in the first four months of the college calendar.[34] There are few solid numbers on how often same-sex assaults happen on college campuses since such assaults are even more likely to be underreported.[35] Prevention should take these patterns seriously.

We also know that drinking is often a factor in sexual assault. In a 2015 fact sheet, the National Institute on Alcohol Abuse and Alcoholism estimated that alcohol was involved in ninety-seven thousand cases of sexual assault and date rape each year among college-age students. Between 50 and 75 percent of reported assaults among students involve heavy drinking. One survey of more than seven thousand students at twenty-two universities showed that women who had consumed large amounts of alcohol were more vulnerable than others.[36]

The issue of the link between alcohol and rape has been confused by the failure to distinguish between the liability model and the forward-looking responsibility model. A University of Michigan website on sexual assault displays this unhelpful confusion. It advises readers that it is a "misconception" that "sexual assault happens when people drink too much" and that "if people drank less, rates of sexual assault would plummet." The site then goes on to say, "The consumption of alcohol does not cause sexual assault. Perpetrators, however, often use alcohol or other drugs as a means to facilitate assault. Like other criminal offenses, sexual assault is often an opportunistic crime, and perpetrators often take the survivor's incapacitation as an opportunity to commit violence."[37] It does not do anyone a favor to suggest, while clarifying that victims are never to blame for rape, that there is not a link between alcohol and sexual assault.

There is a debate about what percentage of rape on campus is committed by serial predators. One well-cited but controversial study notes that of the 6 percent of men who admitted to rape on campus, 63 percent were serial rapists.[38] In a more recent survey of sixteen hundred college men published in the *JAMA (Journal of the American Medical Association) Pediatrics*, the researchers found a higher proportion of men—10.8 percent of the total sample—who would be considered rapists, but far fewer of them—only 25 percent, not 63 percent—said they had committed those acts over multiple college years.[39] These numbers have far-reaching implications for policy and for my argument about responsibility. "Based on this data, if universities tailor their sexual assault intervention strategies to fit the assumption that most rape is being perpetrated by serial offenders, you'll miss three-quarters of the people who are committing rape on college campuses," Kevin Swartout, the author of the *JAMA* study, concluded.[40] A serial rapist problem implies that prosecuting predators and removing them from the population is the solution. The alternative—that many students are potentially capable of coercing a partner to engage in non-consensual sex—would be a better fit for a broad rights-and-responsibilities approach to the issue.[41]

There are anti-rape and sexual assault programs today on some campuses that take a responsibility perspective. Programs focused on men are called "violence prevention," and those focused on women are called "risk reduction." For example, bystander training programs on campus focus on training other students to look out for everyone's safety, with actions as varied as giving someone a safe ride or walk home to confronting directly someone who is engaged in threatening behavior.[42] Bystander training on campus is one important responsibility initiative. One intervention using the bystander approach combined with content designed to shift the social norms within a campus dorm showed a reduction in men's self-reported sexual aggression.[43] The effectiveness of bystander training is still mainly untested, however, and it reserves no clear role for the victim. In general, one survey of the literature concluded that "programming efforts have generally not been successful in reducing sexual violence on college campuses."[44]

The anti-sexual assault program with the best results is a twelve-hour self-defense program teaching freshmen women to identify when they're in a bad situation and how to protect themselves, designed by Charlene Senn, a psychologist at the University of Windsor, Ontario.[45] During the training, Senn hangs up a sign to remind students of their four rights—the rights to have the sex one wants and not to have the sex one doesn't want, to defend oneself, and to speak out when one doesn't like what someone else is doing.[46] Although Senn calls all four of these "rights," we might call the first two "rights" and the second two "responsibilities."

After running the program for a number of years, Senn and colleagues designed a study of 893 college women to test its effectiveness. They reported their findings in the *New England Journal of Medicine*.[47] One group in the experiment was randomly assigned the self-defense training, what the researchers called the EAAA program or resistance training. The control group was given brief exposure to brochures about sexual assault, which are what most universities make available to students. One year after completing the intervention, women in the EAAA program experienced 46 percent fewer completed rapes and 63 percent fewer attempted rapes than women in the control group.[48]

The content of the resistance training is unique and important, and it is not completely captured by the term "self-defense." The first unit of the training (Assess) focuses on teaching young women skills for assessing situations where there might be a risk of sexual assault by male acquaintances and developing problem-solving strategies. Unit 2 (Acknowledge) "assisted women to more quickly acknowledge the danger in situations that have turned coercive, to overcome emotional barriers to resisting the unwanted sexual behavior and to practice resisting verbal coercion." Unit 3 (Act) included two hours of self-defense training.[49]

"What this means in practical terms," Senn explained, "is that enrolling 22 women in the EAAA resistance program would prevent one additional rape from occurring." Not only were rape and attempted rape lower, but the rates of attempted coercion and non-consensual sexual contact were also lower, showing that the resistance training has additional benefits. According to one researcher, "This is the only program that actually decreases the sexual violence women experience for at least one year."[50] While the program was developed for freshmen women, there is no reason it could not be extended to other students.

Forward-looking networked responsibility programs of these types, both bystander training and resistance training, are important tools for addressing sexual assault on campus.

The Harvard Task Force on the Prevention of Sexual Assault recommended that every student receive education about sexual assault and that all resident advisers, tutors, and proctors engage in sexual assault prevention and response training. The training, the report stated, should be used to establish "institutional norms and culture," including as one of its core topics "the responsibility as an individual, community member, and bystander."[51] But not all campus institutions that address sexual assault may be comfortable offering all forms of training. On the Harvard campus, for example, the campus police, not the OSAPR, offer self-defense training (though not the resistance program pioneered by Senn and her colleagues). A staff person from OSAPR described the challenges the staffers face in trying to put the voices and lived-expertise of people who have experienced interpersonal violence at the center of their work while also implementing preventative interventions that may reduce rates of harm:

> Often the most direct prevention and risk-reduction interventions create a dynamic in which those who are most impacted by violence are asked to shoulder the responsibility for stopping it. . . . As a field, this presents an opportunity to think strategically about how to develop partnerships with other community members and agencies who might be in positions to offer programming like self-defense while offices tasked with responding to interpersonal violence offer trainings that explore the social ecology of interactions and build skills and norms that reduce the likelihood of harm occurring.[52]

This sounds like a description of networked responsibility and a moral division of labor, as discussed in chapter 2 above. The crucial issue is that using different means and divisions of labor, universities can do more to exercise their forward-looking responsibilities to prevent sexual assault. By doing so, it appears they would significantly reduce rape, attempted rape, and other non-consensual sexual contact on campus. Survivors and those most impacted by violence can choose to be an essential part of this forward-looking networked responsibility but should not be expected to shoulder a disproportionate share of the burden. This is a good example of what we on campuses around this country can do together to prevent sexual assault.

CONCLUSION

What I have learned while writing this book is that the framework of rights *and* responsibilities is a way of thinking that can be applied to a wide range of human rights issues. While I have tried to illustrate this point through some specific cases, I cannot pretend to do justice to the range of potentially relevant issues.

A problem with the rights-and-responsibilities framework is that there are many rights and thus many responsibilities. It can make people feel so overwhelmed that they don't know where to begin. This is why Young's notion of discretion is so important: we can't all do everything. Yet even Young leaves "discretion" unspecified. We are all socially connected and potentially able to take action on many rights issues. My own modest suggestion is that we take responsibility for issues that we either know and care deeply about or that are unavoidable in our lives. That is what I have done here. This book describes my own quite idiosyncratic set of issues that I know and care about and that came to my attention as ones where a rights-and-responsibilities framework would be fruitful. We each have our idiosyncratic lists of issues.

In this book I have not advocated any particular set of responsibilities but rather the fruitfulness of bringing responsibilities more explicitly back into our discussions of rights. Doing so doesn't solve anything for us, but it gives us new conceptual tools for finding solutions. I believe, as well, that one can speak to these issues from the point of view of a social scientist, asking not only what is right, but also what works— what works to construct new norms and build campaigns, even what works to protest more effectively or diminish sexual assault on campus. We need to take up Weber's ethic of responsibility in the sense of being concerned not only about having the right intentions, but also in thinking about the consequences of our actions.

I encourage you to use this relatively simple framework yourself. When facing a human rights issue, ask yourself not only who are the bearers of rights, but also who are the agents of justice. Who are the multiple actors able to promote the fulfillment of rights? Don't just ask, "Who is to blame?" That is an important issue but not always the most relevant one for implementing many human rights. Ask instead: What together we can do?

Notes

CHAPTER I. WHAT TOGETHER WE CAN DO

1. I am deeply indebted to earlier work on this topic that I have done with Fernando Berdion del Valle, and I thank him for permission to draw on our joint work in this book. See Fernando Berdion del Valle and Kathryn Sikkink, "(Re)Discovering Duties: Individual Responsibilities in the Age of Rights," *Minnesota Journal of International Law* 26, no. 1 (February 2017). Scholars interested in a deeper history of duties and full citations should consult that article. I also draw on my own earlier coauthored work on transnational advocacy networks and on norm dynamics. See Margaret E. Keck and Kathryn Sikkink, *Activists beyond Borders: Advocacy Networks in International Politics* (Ithaca, N.Y.: Cornell University Press, 1998); Martha Finnemore and Kathryn Sikkink, "International Norm Dynamics and Political Change," *International Organization* 52, no. 4 (October 1, 1998): 887–917.

2. Onora O'Neill, *Justice across Boundaries: Whose Obligations?* (Cambridge: Cambridge University Press, 2016).

3. There are important exceptions to this statement, including, for example, Jeremy Waldron, "Dignity, Rights, and Responsibilities," *Arizona State Law Journal* 43 (2011): 1107–36. See also Stephan Parmentier, Hans Werdmölder, and Michaël Merrigan, eds., *Between Rights and Responsibilities: A Fundamental Debate* (Cambridge, Antwerp, and Portland: Intersentia, 2016); Samuel Moyn, "Rights vs. Duties: Reclaiming Civic Balance," *Boston Review*, May 16, 2016; Hakan Altinay, ed., *Global Civics:*

Responsibilities and Rights in an Interdependent World (Washington, D.C.: Brookings Institution Press, 2011); William F. Felice, *The Ethics of Inter-dependence: Global Human Rights and Duties* (Lanham, Md.: Rowman and Littlefield, 2016); Julio Montero, "Human Rights, Personal Responsibility, and Human Dignity: What Are Our Moral Duties to Promote the Universal Realization of Human Rights?," *Human Rights Review* 18, no. 1 (2017): 67–85; Eric R. Boot, *Human Duties and the Limits of Human Rights Discourse* (Cham: Springer International Publishing, 2017), Studies in Global Justice, vol. 17; Makau wa Mutua, "The Banjul Charter and the African Cultural Fingerprint: An Evaluation of the Language of Duties," *Virginia Journal of International Law* 35, no. 2 (1995): 339–80.

4. My work on transitional justice, including Kathryn Sikkink, *The Justice Cascade: How Human Rights Prosecutions Are Changing World Politics* (New York: W. W. Norton, 2011), examined state and individual accountability for mass atrocity, but I have not focused on the kinds of forward-looking responsibility that are the topic of this volume.

5. Iris Marion Young, *Responsibility for Justice* (New York: Oxford University Press, 2011), 9, Oxford Political Philosophy.

6. O'Neill, *Justice across Boundaries*, 167.

7. Mark Blitz, *Duty Bound: Responsibility and American Public Life* (Lanham, Md.: Rowman and Littlefield, 2005), 1.

8. Fred Abrahams, "Healthy for the Long Haul: Building Resilience in Human Rights Workers," Human Rights Watch, April 11, 2017, https://www.hrw.org/news/2017/04/11/healthy-long-haul.

9. Conversation with Paul Korn, September 29, 2018, Cambridge, Massachusetts.

10. Conversations with Jane Mansbridge and Marshall Ganz, Cambridge, Massachusetts.

11. I am indebted to Samuel Moyn for drawing my attention to this duty/rights issue. See also his essay, "Rights vs. Duties."

12. Kathryn Sikkink, "Wake up, Hapless Technology Users," BostonGlobe.com, March 21, 2018, sec. Opinion, https://www.bostonglobe.com/opinion/2018/03/21/wake-hapless-technology-users/8TpT8tqKQZZhchpusBW6IL/story.html.

13. See Natasha Singer, "Just Don't Call It Privacy," *New York Times*, September 23, 2018.

14. See, for example, Geoffrey A. Fowler, "Hands off My Data! 15 Default Privacy Settings You Should Change Right Now," *Washington*

Post, June 1, 2018, https://www.washingtonpost.com/news/the-switch/wp/2018/06/01/hands-off-my-data-15-default-privacy-settings-you-should-change-right-now/.

15. See Joseph S. Nye, "Is Fake News Here to Stay?," *Boston Globe*, December 7, 2018, https://www.bostonglobe.com/opinion/2018/12/07/fake-news-here-stay/Xm7ia1gfcATpVN34J6nU.

16. Young, *Responsibility for Justice*, 153.

17. Christopher Stone, "Should Trees Have Standing?—Toward Legal Rights for Natural Objects," *S. Cal. L. Rev.* 45 (1972), 450, 453–55, for example, has been cited over 2,500 times in articles and related book chapters. See also Cletus Gregor Barié, "Nuevas narrativas constitucionales en Bolivia y Ecuador: El buen vivir y los derechos de la naturaleza," *Latinoamérica: Revista de Estudios Latinoamericanos* 59 (January 1, 2014): 9–40.

18. Marianne Goodland, "Lawsuit: Give the Colorado River the Sames [*sic*] Rights as People, Corporations," *Colorado Springs Gazette*, September 26, 2017, https://gazette.com/lawsuit-give-the-colorado-river-the-sames-rights-as-people/article_427a91f7-608e-5dc3-a7be-1af357bb2a2d.html.

19. See Michael Safi and agencies, "Ganges and Yamuna Rivers Granted Same Legal Rights as Human Beings," *The Guardian*, March 21, 2017, sec. World, https://www.theguardian.com/world/2017/mar/21/ganges-and-yamuna-rivers-granted-same-legal-rights-as-human-beings. The Indian court, in turn, cited a recent New Zealand court decision giving rights to two sacred rivers of the Maori people. Eleanor Ainge Roy, "New Zealand River Granted Same Legal Rights as Human Being," *The Guardian*, March 16, 2017, sec. World, https://www.theguardian.com/world/2017/mar/16/new-zealand-river-granted-same-legal-rights-as-human-being. I thank my brother-in-law, Richard Johnson, for calling this issue to my attention.

20. I am indebted to Joseph Nye for this formulation and for encouraging me to think about collective action problems. In the short space I have here, I cannot even begin to do justice to the vast literature on collective goods.

21. Arguments about the importance of the centralization of the compliance decision have been made by Ellen L. Lutz and Kathryn Sikkink, "International Human Rights Law and Practice in Latin America," *International Organization* 54, no. 3 (2000): 633–59; Thomas Risse, Steve

C. Ropp, and Kathryn Sikkink, eds., *The Persistent Power of Human Rights: From Commitment to Compliance* (Cambridge: Cambridge University Press, 2013), Cambridge Studies in International Relations 126; and Beth Simmons, *Mobilizing for Human Rights: International Law in Domestic Politics* (Cambridge and New York: Cambridge University Press, 2009).

22. Of course, even if the Supreme Court were to outlaw the death penalty, actions by other actors would still be required to implement that decision, such as state law reform to take it off the books, not to mention complex issues of retroactivity for persons in the midst of serving their sentences or undergoing prosecutions for crimes carrying the death penalty at the time the crimes were committed. I thank Martha Minow for alerting me to these issues.

23. Robert William Fogel, *Without Consent or Contract: The Rise and Fall of American Slavery* (New York: W. W. Norton, 1989), 410.

24. Finnemore and Sikkink, "International Norm Dynamics and Political Change."

25. Michael Edison Hayden, "'Alt-Right' Leader Richard Spencer Isn't Sure If Women Should Be Allowed to Vote," *Newsweek*, October 14, 2017, https://www.newsweek.com/alt-right-leader-richard-spencer-isnt-sure-if-women-should-be-allowed-vote-685048.

26. Julianna Pacheco, "Trends—Public Opinion on Smoking and Anti-Smoking Policies," *Public Opinion Quarterly* 75, no. 3 (September 1, 2011): 576–92, https://doi.org/10.1093/poq/nfr031; Institute of Medicine (U.S.) Committee on Secondhand Smoke Exposure and Acute Coronary Events, *The Background of Smoking Bans* (Washington, D.C.: National Academies Press, 2010), https://www.ncbi.nlm.nih.gov/books/NBK219563/.

27. Centers for Disease Control and Prevention, "Cigarette Smoking among U.S. Adults at Lowest Level Ever Recorded: 14% in 2017," November 8, 2018, https://www.cdc.gov/media/releases/2018/p1108-cigarette-smoking-adults.html.

28. See Mutua, "The Banjul Charter and the African Cultural Fingerprint"; Parmentier, Werdmölder, and Merrigan, *Between Rights and Responsibilities*; and Moyn, "Rights vs. Duties."

29. See, for example, Waldron, "Dignity, Rights, and Responsibilities," and Jeremy Waldron, "Special Ties and Natural Duties," *Eweb:125460*, January 1993, https://m.repository.library.georgetown.edu/handle/10822/862355; Mathias Risse, *On Global Justice* (Princeton, N.J.:

Princeton University Press, 2012); Charles R. Beitz, *The Idea of Human Rights* (Oxford and New York: Oxford University Press, 2009); Henry Shue, *Basic Rights: Subsistence, Affluence, and U.S. Foreign Policy*, 2nd ed. (Princeton, N.J.: Princeton University Press, 1996), Princeton Paperbacks; Thomas Winfried Menko Pogge, *World Poverty and Human Rights: Cosmopolitan Responsibilities and Reforms*, 2nd ed. (Cambridge and Malden, Ma.: Polity, 2008); John Tasioulas, "Human Dignity and the Foundations of Human Rights," in *Understanding Human Dignity*, ed. Christopher McCrudden (Oxford: Oxford University Press, 2013), 292, 296–99; Joel Feinberg, "Duties, Rights, and Claims," *American Philosophical Quarterly* 3, no. 2 (1966): 140. Henry Richardson has argued that forward-looking moral responsibility is "largely neglected" and "relatively unfamiliar" to Anglophone analytic philosophy and has developed the concept further in his essay "Institutionally Divided Moral Responsibility," in *Responsibility*, ed. Ellen Frankel Paul, Fred Dycus Miller, and Jeffrey Paul (Cambridge and New York: Cambridge University Press, 1999). For a discussion of the renewal of interest in cosmopolitan duties under international law, see Noah Feldman, "Cosmopolitan Law?," *Yale Law Journal* 116, no. 5 (March 1, 2007): 1022–71.

30. See, for example, O'Neill, *Justice across Boundaries*. I am indebted to Mathias Risse for stressing this point to me.

31. Waldron, "Dignity, Rights, and Responsibilities."

32. Shue, *Basic Rights*. See also Barbara Frey's excellent review of this book, stressing its attention to duties and its relevance today for business and human rights issues: Barbara Frey, "A Review of a Classic Book: Henry Shue, *Basic Rights: Subsistence, Affluence, and U.S. Foreign Policy*," 2nd ed., Princeton Paperbacks (Princeton, N.J.: Princeton University Press, 1996), *Business and Human Rights Journal* 2 (2017): 189–94.

33. Beitz, *The Idea of Human Rights*, 59, 106–9.

34. M. Risse, *On Global Justice*, 213, 231.

35. Pogge, *World Poverty and Human Rights*. I thank Mathias Risse for helping me better understand this argument.

36. François Ost and Sebastien van Drooghenbroeck, "La responsibilidad como cara oculta de los derechos humanos," *Anuario de Derechos Humanos, Nueva Epoca* 5 (2004): 786.

37. Yascha Mounk, *The Age of Responsibility: Luck, Choice, and the Welfare State* (Cambridge, Ma.: Harvard University Press, 2017).

38. I am indebted to my colleague at the Radcliffe Institute, legal scholar Patricia Williams, for taking the time to explain this point of view to me.

39. Mounk, *The Age of Responsibility.*

40. Blitz, *Duty Bound,* 1.

41. See, for example, Boot, *Human Duties and the Limits of Human Rights Discourse.*

42. Mary Ann Glendon, *Rights Talk: The Impoverishment of Political Discourse* (New York: Collier Macmillan, 1991); Jacob Mchangama and Guglielmo Verdirame, "The Danger of Human Rights Proliferation," *Foreign Affairs,* July 24, 2013, https://www.foreignaffairs.com/articles/europe/2013–07–24/danger-human-rights-proliferation; Boot, *Human Duties and the Limits of Human Rights Discourse.*

43. All law students, for example, study a foundational law text on the role of rights and duties—Wesley N. Hohfeld, "Some Fundamental Legal Conceptions as Applied to Judicial Reasoning," *Yale Law Journal* 23 (1913)—which argues that rights and duties are correlative and questions whether legal rights even exist if they are unaccompanied by duties on others. See also Joseph William Singer, "The Legal Rights Debate in Analytical Jurisprudence from Bentham to Hohfeld," *Wisconsin Law Review* 1982 (1982): 975–1199.

44. I thank Christopher McCrudden for directing me to this case and to his work on dignity. See, in particular, Christopher McCrudden, "Human Dignity and Judicial Interpretation of Human Rights," *European Journal of International Law* 19 (2008): 655. On dignity and rights, see also Waldron, "Dignity, Rights, and Responsibilities," and Reva B. Siegel, "Dignity and Sexuality: Claims on Dignity in Transnational Debates over Abortion and Same-Sex Marriage," *International Journal of Constitutional Law* 10, no. 2 (March 2012): 355–79.

45. Julia Davis, "Forbidding Dwarf Tossing: Defending Dignity or Discrimination Based on Size?," *Yearbook of New Zealand Jurisprudence* 9 (2006): 239, 241.

46. This is similar to what Hakan Altinay has called the need for a "global civics." Altinay, ed., *Global Civics.*

CHAPTER 2. LAYING OUT THE THEORETICAL GROUNDWORK

1. Kathryn Sikkink, *Evidence for Hope: Making Human Rights Work in the 21st Century* (Princeton, N.J.: Princeton University Press, 2017), Human Rights and Crimes against Humanity.

2. The philosophical origins of this duty are not clear since the drafters do not cite specific philosophers. It may be related to Kant's writings about "What Is the Enlightenment?" or to German Romantic ideals of individuality, which involve self-development. See, e.g., Steven Lukes, *Individualism* (Oxford: Blackwell, 1973), Key Concepts in the Social Sciences. Another possible origin is that of normative theories running from Aristotle to St. Thomas Aquinas to modern Catholic social doctrine that have exerted a powerful influence within Latin America, in which a key theme is "that man's nature can only be fulfilled within a community." Alfred C. Stepan has called this Latin American tradition "organic statism" in *The State and Society: Peru in Comparative Perspective* (Princeton, N.J.: Princeton University Press, 1978), 29, citing to Aristotle.

3. See, for example, Pauline Maier, *From Resistance to Revolution: Colonial Radicals and the Development of American Opposition to Britain, 1765-1776* (London: Routledge and Kegan Paul, 1973); Gordon S. Wood, *The Creation of the American Republic, 1776-1787* (New York: W. W. Norton, 1972), Norton Library N644; Cass R. Sunstein, "Beyond the Republican Revival," *Yale Law Journal* 97 (1988): 1539-90.

4. Germán Fernández del Castillo, memorandum to his superior, Jaime Torres Bodet, debriefing the events at Bogotá. Archive, Secretaria de Relaciones Exteriores (SRE) de México. Fernández del Castillo refers in particular to Articles 31 and 36 of the Mexican constitution. My thanks to Fernando Berdion de Valle for locating this document.

5. Johannes Morsink, *The Universal Declaration of Human Rights: Origins, Drafting, and Intent* (Philadelphia: University of Pennsylvania Press, 1999), 130, Pennsylvania Studies in Human Rights.

6. Ibid., 249, 247.

7. Onora O'Neill, *Justice across Boundaries: Whose Obligations?* (Cambridge: Cambridge University Press, 2016), 180.

8. Mary Ann Glendon, *A World Made New: Eleanor Roosevelt and the Universal Declaration of Human Rights* (New York: Random House, 2001), xx.

9. Quoted in "E/CN.4/AC.1/SR.3," June 13, 1947, 9, http://daccess-dds-ny.un.org/doc/UNDOC/GEN/NG9/001/03/PDF/NG900103.pdf?OpenElement.

10. See, for example, the discussion of the lack of duties in constitutions from common law countries in Fernando Berdion del Valle and

Kathryn Sikkink, "(Re)Discovering Duties: Individual Responsibilities in the Age of Rights," *Minnesota Journal of International Law* 26, no. 1 (February 2017).

11. Quoted in U.N. Economic and Social Council, July 1, 1947, E/CN.4/21, Annex C, "U.S. Suggestions for Articles to be Incorporated in an International Bill of Rights," p. 41.

12. Mary Ann Glendon, *Rights Talk: The Impoverishment of Political Discourse* (New York: Collier Macmillan, 1991), p. 12.

13. See the discussion of the role of Catholic social thought in Latin American concern with duties in Berdion del Valle and Sikkink, "(Re)Discovering Duties."

14. Makau wa Mutua, "The Banjul Charter and the African Cultural Fingerprint: An Evaluation of the Language of Duties," *Virginia Journal of International Law* 35, no. 2 (1995): 339–80; Mumba Malila, "Individuals' Duties in the African Human Rights Protection System," in *Between Rights and Responsibilities: A Fundamental Debate*, ed. Stephan Parmentier, Hans Werdmölder, and Michaël Merrigan (Cambridge, Antwerp, and Portland: Intersentia, 2016), 195 and 202.

15. Malila, "Individuals' Duties in the African Human Rights Protection System," 217 and 225.

16. Chapter 2 of the charter, paragraph 1 of Article 27.

17. For notable exceptions, see Mutua, "The Banjul Charter and the African Cultural Fingerprint"; Jordan J. Paust, "The Other Side of Right: Private Duties under Human Rights Law," *Harvard Human Rights Journal* 5 (1992): 56; Malila, "Individuals' Duties in the African Human Rights Protection System."

18. These include the Trieste Declaration of Human Duties by the International Council of Human Duties in 1993; the Universal Declaration of Human Responsibilities, launched by a group of former world leaders calling themselves the InterAction Council, in 1997; the Declaration on the Responsibilities of the Present Generations towards Future Generations, adopted by the General Conference of UNESCO in 1997; the Valencia Declaration of Human Duties and Responsibilities by a high-level group chaired by Richard J. Goldstone under the auspices of the City of Valencia and UNESCO in 1998; Recommendation 1401 of the Parliamentary Assembly by the Council of Europe on Education in the Responsibilities of the Individual in 1998; Resolution 91 on Re-

sponsible Citizenship and Participation in Public Life by the Congress of Local and Regional Authorities of the Council of Europe in 2000; the pre-draft of the Declaration on Human Social Responsibilities of the Special Rapporteur of the U.N. Commission on Human Rights in 2003; and Resolution 1845 of the Parliamentary Assembly of the Council of Europe on Fundamental Rights and Responsibilities in 2011; Parmentier, Werdmölder, and Merrigan, *Between Rights and Responsibilities*, 3–4.

19. InterAction Council, "A Universal Declaration of Human Responsibilities," September 1, 1997.

20. Amartya Sen, *Human Rights and Asian Values* (New York: Carnegie Council on Ethics and International Affairs, 1997), 10, http://rarre.org/documents/sen/Sen-%20Human%20Rights%20and%20 Asian%20Values.pdf.

21. InterAction Council, "A Universal Declaration of Human Responsibilities."

22. Ibid.

23. Ben Saul, "In the Shadow of Human Rights: Human Duties, Obligations, and Responsibilities," *Columbia Human Rights Law Review* 32 (2001): 565.

24. Siobhán Mullally, *Gender, Culture and Human Rights: Reclaiming Universalism* (London: Bloomsbury Publishing, 2006), 8.

25. Amnesty International and International Secretariat, *Muddying the Waters: The Draft "Universal Declaration of Human Responsibilities": No Complement to Human Rights* (London: Amnesty International, International Secretariat, 1998).

26. Personal email communication from William Schulz, October 15, 2018. Used with permission.

27. Ibid.

28. "Declaration on the Right and Responsibility," accessed September 23, 2015, http://www.unhchr.ch/huridocda/huridoca.nsf/(Symbol)/ A.RES.53.144.En?OpenDocument.

29. "Declaration on the Right and Responsibility of Individuals, Groups and Organs of Society to Promote and Protect Universally Recognized Human Rights and Fundamental Freedoms: Resolution / Adopted by the General Assembly," Refworld, accessed September 30, 2015, http://www.refworld.org/docid/3b00f54c14.html.

30. Charles R. Beitz, *The Idea of Human Rights* (Oxford and New York: Oxford University Press, 2009), 102.

31. Jack Donnelly, *Universal Human Rights in Theory and Practice*, 2nd ed. (Ithaca, N.Y.: Cornell University Press, 2003), 40.

32. Martha Finnemore and Kathryn Sikkink, "International Norm Dynamics and Political Change," *International Organization* 52, no. 4 (October 1, 1998): 887–917.

33. Emanuel Adler and Vincent Pouliot, *International Practices* (Cambridge and New York: Cambridge University Press, 2011), 6, Cambridge Studies in International Relations, vol. 119.

34. Adler and Pouliot, *International Practices*, 7. On practices, see also Rebecca Abers and Margaret Keck, *Practical Authority: Agency and Institutional Change in Brazilian Water Politics* (New York: Oxford University Press, 2015).

35. See, however, Beth A. Simmons, *Mobilizing for Human Rights: International Law in Domestic Politics* (Cambridge and New York: Cambridge University Press, 2009); Thomas Risse, Steve C. Ropp, and Kathryn Sikkink, eds., *The Persistent Power of Human Rights: From Commitment to Compliance* (Cambridge: Cambridge University Press, 2013), Cambridge Studies in International Relations 126.

36. Joel Feinberg, "Duties, Rights, and Claims," *American Philosophical Quarterly* 3, no. 2 (1966): 140.

37. Ibid., 140–41. So, for example, John Ruggie, who developed the Guiding Principles for Business and Human Rights, made a conscious decision to refer to a state *duty* to protect human rights and a corporate *responsibility*. He wrote, "My use of the term 'responsibility' was intended to signal that it differs from legal duties" (John Gerard Ruggie, *Just Business: Multinational Corporations and Human Rights*, 1st ed. [New York: W. W. Norton, 2013], 91, Amnesty International Global Ethics Series). Iris Young wrote, "When we have a duty, moral rules specify what it is we are supposed to do: for example, 'Honor thy father and thy mother.' Responsibility, however, while no less obligatory, is more open as to what actions it calls for" (Iris Marion Young, *Responsibility for Justice* [New York: Oxford University Press, 2011], 143).

38. Eric R. Boot, *Human Duties and the Limits of Human Rights Discourse* (Cham: Springer International Publishing, 2017), 31, Studies in Global Justice, vol. 17.

39. Elizabeth Jelin, "Citizenship Revisited: Solidarity, Responsibility, and Rights," in *Constructing Democracy: Human Rights, Citizenship, and Society in Latin America,* ed. Elizabeth Jelin and Eric Hershberg (Boulder, Colo.: Westview Press, 1996), 106.

40. Mark Blitz, *Duty Bound: Responsibility and American Public Life* (Lanham, Md.: Rowman and Littlefield, 2005), 1. But a search of the content of the Federalist Papers reveals that the term *responsibility* is used rarely and that *duty* is the far more common term.

41. My thanks to Catherine Zhang, Hannah Ellery, and Roshni Chakraborty for research on the prevalence of these concepts.

42. Yascha Benjamin Mounk, "The Age of Responsibility: On the Role of Choice, Luck and Personal Responsibility in Contemporary Politics and Philosophy" (PhD diss., Harvard University, 2015).

43. Charlotte Walker-Said and John Dunham Kelly, eds., *Corporate Social Responsibility?: Human Rights in the New Global Economy* (Chicago: University of Chicago Press, 2015); Olufemi Amao, *Corporate Social Responsibility, Human Rights and the Law: Multinational Corporations in Developing Countries* (Milton Park, Abingdon, Oxon, and New York: Routledge, 2011), Routledge Research in Corporate Law; John Ruggie, "Protect, Respect and Remedy: A Framework for Business and Human Rights," *Innovations* 3, no. 2 (2008): 189–212; Jernej Letnar Cernic and Tara Van Ho, eds., *Human Rights and Business: Direct Corporate Accountability for Human Rights* (Oisterwijk, The Netherlands: Wolf Legal Publishers, 2015).

44. Francis Mading Deng, *Sovereignty as Responsibility: Conflict Management in Africa* (Washington, D.C.: Brookings Institution Press, 1996); Gareth J. Evans, *The Responsibility to Protect: Ending Mass Atrocity Crimes Once and for All* (Washington, D.C.: Brookings Institution Press, 2008).

45. Lavanya Rajamani, *Differential Treatment in International Environmental Law* (Oxford: Oxford University Press, 2006), Oxford Monographs in International Law.

46. Ruggie, *Just Business.*

47. Henry Richardson, "Institutionally Divided Moral Responsibility," in *Responsibility*, ed. Ellen Frankel Paul, Fred Dycus Miller, and Jeffrey Paul (Cambridge and New York: Cambridge University Press, 1999); Young, *Responsibility for Justice.*

48. Young, *Responsibility for Justice*, 2011.

49. Ellen Frankel Paul, Fred Dycus Miller, and Jeffrey Paul, *Responsibility* (Cambridge: Cambridge University Press, 1999), vii.

50. Kathryn Sikkink, *The Justice Cascade: How Human Rights Prosecutions Are Changing World Politics* (New York: W. W. Norton, 2011).

51. I am particularly indebted to my colleague at the Radcliffe Institute, the writer and law professor Patricia Williams, for talking to me about her ideas about why *responsibility* is not the right term. An example of this particular use of the term is discussed by Yascha Mounk, "Democrats Copied the GOP's Politics of 'Personal Responsibility,' and It Hurt America," *Washington Post*, May 26, 2017, https://www.washingtonpost.com/posteverything/wp/2017/05/26/democrats-copied-the-gops-politics-of-personal-responsibility-and-it-hurt-america/?noredirect=on&utm_term=.d7560f913acc.

52. Max Weber, *Max Weber: Selections in Translation* (Cambridge and New York: Cambridge University Press, 1978), 218.

53. Ibid., 212.

54. Ibid., 215.

55. See Peter Singer, *The Most Good You Can Do: How Effective Altruism Is Changing Ideas about Living Ethically* (New Haven: Yale University Press, 2015), Castle Lectures in Ethics, Politics, and Economics.

56. Joseph Nye, *Do Morals Matter? Presidents and Foreign Policy from FDR to Trump* (Oxford: Oxford University Press, forthcoming).

57. W. G. Runciman, "Introduction," in *Max Weber: Selections in Translation* (Cambridge and New York: Cambridge University Press, 1978), 209.

58. Seth Wynes and Kimberly A. Nicholas, "The Climate Mitigation Gap: Education and Government Recommendations Miss the Most Effective Individual Actions," *Environmental Research Letters* 12, no. 7 (July 1, 2017): 1.

59. Hannah Arendt, *Eichmann in Jerusalem: A Report on the Banality of Evil*, rev. and enl. ed. (New York: Penguin Books, 1976), 179.

60. For an overview of this controversy and Arendt's reaction to it, see the chapter "Cura Posterior: Eichmann in Jerusalem (1961–1965)" in Elisabeth Young-Bruehl, *Hannah Arendt: For Love of the World*, 2nd ed. (New Haven: Yale University Press, 2004).

61. Arendt, *Eichmann in Jerusalem*, 179.

62. Young, *Responsibility for Justice*, in her chapter 3 ("Guilt vs. Responsibility"), develops this distinction in Arendt's work and applies it to *Eichmann in Jerusalem*.

63. Young, *Responsibility for Justice*, 75–76. Young argues that although Arendt says political responsibility "derives simply from common membership in a nation," Arendt's understanding of political responsibility is more complex and also includes a duty "for individuals to take public stands about actions and events that affect broad masses of people, and to try to organize collective action to prevent massive harm or foster institutional change for the better." Young then draws on this broader understanding of responsibility as she crafts her own social connection model.

64. Mathias Risse, *On Global Justice* (Princeton, N.J.: Princeton University Press, 2012).

65. Young, *Responsibility for Justice*, 167.

66. This paragraph draws on O'Neill's discussion of agents of justice in *Justice across Boundaries*, chapter 11, of 177–92. If we read just parts of this book—for example, O'Neill's essay "The Dark Side of Human Rights"—we might think that O'Neill uses the concept of obligation mainly as a way to critique rights. But read in the context of other essays collected in this book, we see O'Neill as a theorist simultaneously stressing rights *and* obligations and seeing the networked responsibilities of diverse actors as essential for the implementation of human rights.

67. O'Neill, *Justice across Boundaries*, 40.

68. Mounk, "The Age of Responsibility," 237.

69. Richardson, "Institutionally Divided Moral Responsibility."

70. Young, *Responsibility for Justice*, 143.

71. Blitz, *Duty Bound*, 17.

72. Young, *Responsibility for Justice*, 143–47.

73. Richardson, "Institutionally Divided Moral Responsibility," 248.

74. Robert O. Keohane and David G. Victor, "The Regime Complex for Climate Change," *Perspectives on Politics* 9, no. 1 (March 15, 2011): 7–23.

75. Http://time.com/collection/davos-2019/5502592/china-social-credit-score/.

76. Roxane Gay, "Ask Roxane: Am I Terrible for Not Doing More?" *New York Times*, April 22, 2018, SR4.

77. Richardson, "Institutionally Divided Moral Responsibility," 249.

78. Margaret E. Keck and Kathryn Sikkink, *Activists beyond Borders: Advocacy Networks in International Politics* (Ithaca, N.Y.: Cornell University Press, 1998), 46.

79. See, for example, Michael Ignatieff, *Human Rights as Politics and Idolatry* (Princeton, N.J.: Princeton University Press, 2001), University Center for Human Values Series.

80. Article 29 (7) of the Banjul Charter. The case, Kasha Nabagesera & 3 Others v. Attorney General & Another, is discussed in Eric Gitari, "Criminalization of Homosexuality and Constitutional Rights," LL.M. Long Paper, draft, March 23, 2018, p. 26.

CHAPTER 3. GLOBAL RIGHTS AND RESPONSIBILITIES

1. Dejusticia, "Acción de tutela," January 29, 2018, https://cdn.De justicia.org/wp-content/uploads/2018/01/TutelaCambioClim%C3% Artico.pdf?x54537&x54537&x54537. Filed with the Tribunal Superior del Distrito Judicial de Bogota—Sala Civil.

2. Michael Gerrard as quoted in César Rodríguez Garavito, "Here Is How Litigation for the Planet Won in Colombia," *Dejusticia* (blog), May 7, 2018, https://www.Dejusticia.org/en/asi-se-gano-en-colombia-un-litigio-por-el-planeta/.

3. This paragraph draws extensively on Rodríguez Garavito, "Here Is How Litigation for the Planet Won in Colombia."

4. "Help Us Build the Intergenerational Pact for the Amazon," *Dejusticia* (blog), April 27, 2018, https://www.Dejusticia.org/en/ayudanos-a-construir-el-pacto-intergeneracional-por-la-amazonia/.

5. See, for example, Augustin Fragnière, "Climate Change and Individual Duties," *Wiley Interdisciplinary Reviews: Climate Change* 7, no. 6 (November 1, 2016): 798–814. Other scholars feel that conceptions of individual duties are inadequate. See, for example, Kok-Chor Tan, "Individual Duties of Climate Justice under Non-Ideal Conditions," *Climate Change and Justice*, 2015.

6. Simon Caney, "Two Kinds of Climate Justice: Avoiding Harm and Sharing Burdens," *Journal of Political Philosophy* 22, no. 2 (2014): 125.

7. Simon P. James, "Climate Change," in Simon P. James, *Environmental Philosophy: An Introduction* (Cambridge, UK, and Malden, Ma.: Polity Press, 2015), 142.

8. Marion Hourdequin, "Climate Change and Individual Responsibility: A Reply to Johnson," *Environmental Values* 20, no. 2 (2011): 157–62.

9. Simo Kyllönen, "Climate Change, No-Harm Principle, and Moral Responsibility of Individual Emitters," *Journal of Applied Philosophy*, November 1, 2016, 7.

10. Ibid.

11. Seth Wynes and Kimberly A. Nicholas, "The Climate Mitigation Gap: Education and Government Recommendations Miss the Most Effective Individual Actions," *Environmental Research Letters* 12, no. 7 (July 1, 2017): 1.

12. Fragnière, "Climate Change and Individual Duties," 807.

13. You can calculate your carbon footprint on various websites. See, for example, https://www.carbonfootprint.com/calculator.aspx.

14. See, for example, Martha Finnemore and Kathryn Sikkink, "International Norm Dynamics and Political Change," *International Organization* 52, no. 4 (October 1, 1998): 887–917; Cass R. Sunstein, "Social Norms and Social Roles," *Columbia Law Review* 96, no. 4 (May 1996): 903–68; Robert William Fogel, *Without Consent or Contract: The Rise and Fall of American Slavery* (New York: W. W. Norton, 1989); Margaret E. Keck and Kathryn Sikkink, *Activists beyond Borders: Advocacy Networks in International Politics* (Ithaca, N.Y.: Cornell University Press, 1998).

15. Aaron Huertas, "Dear Humans, Industry, Not Your Activities, Is Causing Climate Change," *Huffington Post* (blog), April 7, 2015, https://www.huffingtonpost.com/aaron-huertas/dear-humans-industry-is-c_b_7017470.html.

16. I am indebted to William Clark for helping me think more effectively about these issues.

17. "Transportation Is the Biggest Source of U.S. Emissions," Climate Central, November 21, 2017, http://www.climatecentral.org/gallery/graphics/transportation-is-the-biggest-source-of-us-emissions; "Power Sector Carbon Dioxide Emissions Fall below Transportation Sector Emissions," U.S. Energy Information Administration, January 19, 2017, https://www.eia.gov/todayinenergy/detail.php?id=34192.

18. Wynes and Nicholas, "The Climate Mitigation Gap," 1.

19. Ibid.

20. David Roberts, "The Best Way to Reduce Your Personal Carbon Emissions: Don't Be Rich," *Vox* (blog), December 26, 2017, https://www.vox.com/energy-and-environment/2017/7/14/15963544/climate-change-individual-choices.

21. Quoted in Jonathan Shaw, "Eating for the Environment," *Harvard Magazine*, February 9, 2017, https://harvardmagazine.com/2017/03/eating-for-the-environment.

22. Ibid.

23. Jessica Nihlén Fahlquist, "Moral Responsibility for Environmental Problems—Individual or Institutional?," *Journal of Agricultural and Environmental Ethics* 22, no. 2 (2009): 111.

24. Roberts, "The Best Way to Reduce Your Personal Carbon Emissions."

25. Ana Swanson, "You Might Be among the Richest People in the World and Not Realize It," *Washington Post*, January 21, 2016, https://www.washingtonpost.com/news/wonk/wp/2016/01/21/you-might-be-among-the-richest-people-in-the-world-and-not-realize-it/?utm_term=.280a77309feb.

26. "Global Inequality," Inequality.org, accessed July 20, 2018, https://inequality.org/facts/global-inequality/.

27. Tess Riley, "Just 100 Companies Responsible for 71% of Global Emissions, Study Says," *The Guardian*, July 10, 2017, sec. Guardian Sustainable Business, https://www.theguardian.com/sustainable-business/2017/jul/10/100-fossil-fuel-companies-investors-responsible-71-global-emissions-cdp-study-climate-change.

28. Joseph Nye, "Protecting Democracy in an Era of Cyber Information War," *Governance in an Emerging New World*, Fall Series, issue 318, November 13, 2018, Hoover Institution, https://www.hoover.org/research/protecting-democracy-era-cyber-information-war.

29. Thanks to Joseph Nye for comments on this section and for suggesting this vaccination metaphor.

30. Adam Conner, interviewed by Hannah Ellery, Cambridge, Ma., April 23, 2018.

31. See Joseph Nye, "Is Fake News Here to Stay?" *Boston Globe*, December 7, 2018, https://www.bostonglobe.com/opinion/2018/12/07/fake-news-here-stay/Xm7ia1gfcATpVN34J6nU.

32. Nye, "Protecting Democracy."

33. Maeve McDonagh, "The Right to Information in International Human Rights Law," *Human Rights Law Review* 13, no. 1 (March 1, 2013): 25–55, https://doi.org/10.1093/hrlr/ngs045.

34. Iris Marion Young, *Responsibility for Justice* (New York: Oxford University Press, 2011), 153–66, Oxford Political Philosophy.

35. Ibid., 169.

36. Comments by Jane Mansbridge on an early draft chapter of this book.

37. Siva Vaidhyanathan, "Don't Delete Facebook. Do Something about It," *New York Times*, March 24, 2018, sec. Opinion, https://www.nytimes.com/2018/03/24/opinion/sunday/delete-facebook-does-not-fix-problem.html.

CHAPTER 4. NATIONAL RIGHTS AND RESPONSIBILITIES

1. Iris Marion Young, *Responsibility for Justice* (New York: Oxford University Press, 2011). My thanks to William Frucht for drawing my attention to the issues of student privilege.

2. Linz says legitimacy "is the belief that, in spite of shortcomings and failures, the existing political institutions are better than others that could be established, and that they therefore can demand obedience" (Juan J. Linz, *The Breakdown of Democratic Regimes: Crisis, Breakdown, and Reequilibration* [Baltimore: Johns Hopkins University Press, 1978]).

3. Churchill in House of Commons, November 11, 1947, quoting an unknown predecessor. From Winston Churchill and Richard M. Langworth, *Churchill by Himself: The Definitive Collection of Quotations*, 1st ed. (New York: Public Affairs, 2008), 574.

4. Linz, *The Breakdown of Democratic Regimes*, 18.

5. Scott Mainwaring and Aníbal Pérez-Liñán, *Democracies and Dictatorships in Latin America: Emergence, Survival, and Fall* (New York: Cambridge University Press, 2013).

6. Elizabeth Jelin, "¿Cómo construir ciudadanía? Una visión desde abajo," *Revista Europea de Estudios Latinoamericanos y del Caribe / European Review of Latin American and Caribbean Studies*, no. 55 (1993): 21–37.

7. Leftists found new meaning in the words of Che Guevara, who said that "democracy cannot consist solely of elections that are nearly always fictitious and managed by rich landowners and professional politicians, but rather it lies in the right of the citizens to determine their

own destiny" (Che Guevara, *Venceremos!: The Speeches and Writings* [New York: Simon and Schuster, 1968], sec. On Growth and Capitalism).

8. This goal is shared by Democracy Works, the organization behind the TurboVote project. "The TurboVote Challenge," accessed August 18, 2018, http://democracy.works/challenge.

9. Peter Levine, "Getting to 80% Voter Turnout," *Peter Levine* (blog), May 3, 2018, http://peterlevine.ws/?p=19911. For these graphs, Levine relies on data from the United States Elections project, "National General Election VEP Turnout Rates, 1789–Present," United States Elections Project, June 11, 2014, http://www.electproject.org/national-1789-present.

10. All the material in this and the remaining paragraphs in this section is drawn from Nancy Thomas et al., "Democracy Counts: A Report on U.S. College and University Student Voting," Tufts University, Jonathan M. Tisch College of Civic Life, Institute for Democracy and Higher Education, 2017, https://idhe.tufts.edu/sites/default/files/NSLVE%20Report%202012–2016_1.pdf.

11. Alexander Coppock and Donald P. Green, "Is Voting Habit Forming? New Evidence from Experiments and Regression Discontinuities," *American Journal of Political Science* 60, no. 4 (2016): 1044–62, https://doi.org/10.1111/ajps.12210.

12. Thomas et al., "Democracy Counts: A Report from U.S. College and University Student Voting."

13. Phone interview with Nancy Thomas, October 11, 2018.

14. National Study of Learning, Voting, and Engagement, "NSLVE Campus Report, Harvard University," released only to Harvard.

15. Ibid.

16. Interview with Seth Flaxman, Cambridge, Ma., August 29, 2018.

17. "TurboVote: 'Netflix' for Voter Registration," *Harvard Magazine*, September 13, 2011, https://harvardmagazine.com/2011/09/kennedy-school-alumni-launch-turbovote.

18. Ibid.

19. Flaxman quoted in ibid.

20. See Democracy Works website at https://democracy.works/.

21. "TurboVote."

22. Http://iop.harvard.edu/get-involved/community-action.

23. Skype interview with Austin Sowa, March 2, 2018.

24. Ibid.

25. Ibid.

26. Ibid.

27. From the 2008 reauthorization of the Higher Education Act, SEC. 487. [20 U.S.C. 1094].

28. This paragraph is drawn from a short case study by Democracy Works, "Integrating TurboVote into an Online Pre-Semester Process," Harvard Institute of Politics, Summer 2017, 1–7.

29. Faust quoted in "TurboVote."

30. Democracy Works, "Integrating TurboVote into an Online Pre-Semester Process."

31. Phone interview with Nancy Thomas, October 11, 2018.

32. Interview with Derek Paulhus, Cambridge, Ma., March 24, 2018.

CHAPTER 5. WHAT DO THE STUDENTS THINK?

1. There are proposals for formally measuring the responsibility to vote. See Andre Blais and Carol Galais, "Measuring the Civic Duty to Vote: A Proposal," *Electoral Studies* 41 (2015): 60–69. Our efforts to ascertain student attitudes were far more informal, and we did not administer a survey to students as part of the focus groups.

2. The size of our focus groups did not permit any quantitative analysis, but the groups still yielded rich qualitative data about behaviors, feelings, and attitudes.

3. Harvard House Focus Group #4.

4. Harvard House Focus Group #2.

5. Harvard House Focus Group #2.

6. Harvard House Focus Group #1.

7. Harvard House Focus Group #1.

8. Harvard House Focus Group #4.

9. Harvard House Focus Group #4.

10. Harvard House Focus Group #1.

11. Harvard House Focus Group #1.

12. Harvard House Focus Group #2.

13. Harvard House Focus Group #3.

14. Harvard House Focus Group #2.

15. Https://sos.tn.gov/products/elections/absentee-voting.

16. Kayla Tarrant, "The Suppression of Student Votes Is a Real Thing," *Huffington Post* (blog), November 2, 2016, https://www.huffing tonpost.com/entry/the-suppression-of-student-votes-is-a-real-thing_ us_581a18d9e4b0f1c7d77c94a9.

17. Harvard House Focus Group #1.

18. Harvard House Focus Group #4.

19. Harvard House Focus Group #1.

20. Harvard House Focus Group #3.

21. Harvard House Focus Group #4.

22. All comments in this paragraph come from Harvard House Focus Group #1.

23. See, for example, the findings of the Institute of Politics Spring 2018 Youth Poll, http://iop.harvard.edu/spring-2018-poll.

24. Harvard House Focus Group #4.

25. Harvard House Focus Group #3.

26. Harvard House Focus Group #1.

27. Harvard House Focus Group #4.

28. One study found that sending mail indicating that voting is a civic duty increased turnout by only 1 percent and was much less effective than other forms of mobilization. Alan S. Gerber, Donald P. Green, and Christopher W. Larimer, "Social Pressure and Voter Turnout: Evidence from a Large-Scale Field Experiment," *American Political Science Review* 102, no. 1 (February 2008): 38.

29. See Alan S. Gerber and Todd Rogers, "Descriptive Social Norms and Motivation to Vote: Everybody's Voting and So Should You," *Journal of Politics* 71, no. 1 (January 2009). For a survey of the psychological literature as it relates to student voters, see D. J. Nen, Jess Leifer, and Anthony Barrows, "Graduating Students into Voters: Overcoming the Psychological Barriers Faced by Student Voters," produced by Ideas 42 and the Foundation for Civic Leadership, April 2016.

30. For example, voting parties and campus-community partnerships have been effective and cost-effective at increasing turnout; parties in particular increased turnout by 6.5 percent. See Elizabeth M. Addonizio, Donald P. Green, and James M. Glaser, "Putting the Party Back into Politics: An Experiment Testing Whether Election Day Festivals Increase Voter Turnout," *PS: Political Science and Politics* 40, no. 4 (October 2007): 723.

31. The recent book by Francis Moore Lappé and Adam Eichen, *Daring Democracy: Igniting Power, Meaning, and Connection for the America We Want* (Boston: Beacon Press, 2017), is instructive reading for anyone interested in the scope of the democracy movement in the United States, as well as the challenges it faces.

32. Interview with Teddy Landis, Cambridge, Ma., October 25, 2018.

33. Molly McCafferty, "Bacow, Khurana Call for Civic Engagement in Challenging Times at Convocation," *Harvard Crimson*, September 4, 2018, http://www.thecrimson.com/article/2018/9/4/bacow-freshman-convocation/; Kristine Guillaume, "Harvard President Bacow Urges Students to Vote in Email Headlined 'Democracy,'" *Harvard Crimson*, October 3, 2018, http://www.thecrimson.com/article/2018/10/3/bacow-democracy/; Simone Chu and Abigail Simon, "Why the Hell Don't Harvard Students Vote?," *Harvard Crimson*, October 11, 2018, https://www.thecrimson.com/article/2018/10/11/why-the-hell-dont-harvard-students-vote/.

34. Based on a comparison of event calendars at IOP and at other public policy schools around the country. We accessed the events calendars on the websites of public policy schools across the country (Texas A&M University's Bush School, University of California at Berkeley's Goldman School, and the University of Michigan's Ford School) and counted all events related to elections and/or voting in 2014, 2016, and 2018. We chose schools from diverse states in terms of geography and political affiliation.

35. Quoted in Simone Chu, "Harvard Votes Challenge Calls on Undergrads to Beat Yale—at the Ballot Box," *Harvard Crimson*, October 10, 2018, http://www.thecrimson.com/article/2018/10/10/harvard-yale-vote/.

36. Roshni Chakraborty, memo to Kathryn Sikkink on voting at Harvard, December 14, 2018.

37. Interview with Emily Brother, Cambridge, Ma., October 3, 2018.

38. Interview with a senior at Harvard College, Cambridge, Ma., October 30, 2018.

39. Tufts University, "Democracy Counts: A Report from U.S. Colleges and University Student Voting," https://idhe.tufts.edu/sites/default/files/NSLVE%20Report%202012–2016_1.pdf.

40. Center for Information and Research on Civic Learning and Engagement (CIRCLE), "Young People Dramatically Increase Their Turnout to 31%, Shape 2018 Midterm Elections," https://civicyouth.org/young-people-dramatically-increase-their-turnout-31-percent-shape-2018-midterm-elections/, accessed January 15, 2019.

41. CIRCLE, "Young People Dramatically Increase their Turnout."

CHAPTER 6. CHANGING NORMS AND PRACTICES

1. On norm definitions and dynamics, see Martha Finnemore and Kathryn Sikkink, "International Norm Dynamics and Political Change," *International Organization* 52, no. 4 (October 1, 1998): 887–917.

2. On the role of schemas in voter mobilization, see Lisa Garcia Bedolla and Melissa Michelson, *Mobilizing Inclusion: Transforming the Electorate through Get-Out-the-Vote Campaigns* (New Haven: Yale University Press, 2012).

3. My thanks to Joseph Nye for this insight.

4. This is one of the most basic contributions of the constructivist approach to international relations. See Martha Finnemore, *National Interests in International Society* (Ithaca, N.Y.: Cornell University Press, 1996).

5. Harvard House Focus Group #4.

6. The classic text on the topic is Anthony Downs, *An Economic Theory of Democracy* (New York: Harper, 1957).

7. Alvin I. Goldman, "Why Citizens Should Vote: A Causal Responsibility Approach," *Social Philosophy and Policy* 16, no. 2 (1999): 201–17.

8. David Knoke, "Networks of Political Action: Towards Theory Construction," *Social Forces* 68, no. 4 (1990): 1058, as cited in Bedolla and Michelson, *Mobilizing Inclusion*.

9. Harold Koh comments, Yale University, October 11, 2017. On this issue, see also Heather Lardy, "Is There a Right Not to Vote?," *Oxford Journal of Legal Studies* 24, no. 2 (2004): 303–21, https://doi.org/10.1093/ojls/24.2.303.

10. I thank my editor, William Frucht, for this insight.

11. In the case of the right to free speech, the Supreme Court has ruled that there is a "concomitant freedom not to speak publicly," but it

has not made this argument with regard to the core duties of citizenship, such as the duty to serve on juries, pay taxes, provide military service, or vote. See *Estate of Hemingway v. Random House, Inc* 23 N.Y.2d 341 (N.Y. 1968).

12. See Colin Wight, *Agents, Structures and International Relations: Politics as Ontology* (Cambridge: Cambridge University Press, 2006), 207. For a discussion about agency in international relations, see my unpublished article, "Beyond the Justice Cascade: How Agentic Constructivism Can Help Explain Change in International Politics," https://www.princeton.edu/politics/about/file-repository/public/Agentic-Constructivism-paper-sent-to-the-Princeton-IR-Colloquium.pdf.

13. For a lucid overview of all these barriers, see Frances Moore Lappé and Adam Eichen, *Daring Democracy: Igniting Power, Meaning, and Connection for the America We Want* (Boston: Beacon Press, 2017). For detailed research on the power of money in the U.S. political system, see Jane Mayer, *Dark Money: The Hidden History of the Billionaires behind the Rise of the Radical Right*, 1st ed. (New York: Doubleday, 2016).

14. Hannah Arendt, *Eichmann in Jerusalem: A Report on the Banality of Evil*, rev. and enl. ed. (New York: Penguin Books, 1976), 297.

15. The impact of personal contact is seen in the fact that door-to-door canvassing involving face-to-face contact increases turnout much more than do mail, email, or telephone calls and is especially effective among voters with a low propensity to vote. Kevin Arceneaux and David W. Nickerson, "Who Is Mobilized to Vote? A Re-Analysis of 11 Field Experiments," *American Journal of Political Science* 53, no. 1 (December 24, 2008): 1–16. See also Marshall Ganz, "Motor Voter or Motivated Voter?" *American Prospect*, October 1996, http://prospect.org/article/motor-voter-or-motivated-voter.

16. Lisa Bedolla, Marisa Abrajano, and Jane Junn, "Insight: Testing New Technologies in Mobilizing Voters of Color" (James Irvine Foundation, October 2015); Neil Malhotra et al., "Text Messages as Mobilization Tools: The Conditional Effect of Habitual Voting and Election Salience," *American Politics Research* 39, no. 4 (2011): 664–81; Lauren Deschamps Keane and David W. Nickerson, "When Reports Depress Rather Than Inspire: A Field Experiment Using Age Cohorts as Reference Groups," *Journal of Political Marketing* 14, no. 4 (October 2, 2015): 381–90; David W. Nickerson, "Does Email Boost Turnout?," *Quarterly*

Journal of Political Science 2, no. 4 (January 30, 2008): 369–79; Costas Panagopoulos and Donald P. Green, "Spanish-Language Radio Advertisements and Latino Voter Turnout in the 2006 Congressional Elections: Field Experimental Evidence," *Political Research Quarterly* 64, no. 3 (September 1, 2011); Sarah Niebler, Jacob Neiheisel, and Matthew Holleque, "By Ground or by Air? Voter Mobilization during the United States' 2008 Presidential Campaign," *Journal of Elections, Public Opinion and Parties* 28, no. 1 (January 2, 2018): 78–104.

17. Quote from Marshall Ganz, "Voters in the Crosshairs," *American Prospect*, Winter 1994. See also Bedolla and Michelson, *Mobilizing Inclusion*.

18. Alexander Keyssar, *The Right to Vote: The Contested History of Democracy in the United States* (New York: Basic Books, 2000).

19. U.S. Environmental Protection Agency, "America Recycles Day 2017," https://www.epa.gov/recycle/america-recycles-day-2017, accessed August 28, 2018.

20. Archon Fung, email communication, December 3, 2018.

CHAPTER 7. THE RIGHTS AND RESPONSIBILITIES
FRAMEWORK ON CAMPUS

1. Kathryn Sikkink, *Evidence for Hope: Making Human Rights Work in the 21st Century* (Princeton, N.J.: Princeton University Press, 2017), Human Rights and Crimes against Humanity.

2. Max Weber, *Politics as a Vocation*, vol. 3 (Philadelphia: Fortress Press, 1965), Social Ethics.

3. Iris Marion Young, *Responsibility for Justice* (New York: Oxford University Press, 2011), 143, 144, Oxford Political Philosophy.

4. Nashaw Bawah, "Appalachian State Students Greeted by White Supremacy Banner," *USA Today*, August 24, 2017, https://www.usatoday.com/story/college/2017/08/24/appalachian-state-students-greeted-by-white-supremacy-banner/37435193/.

5. Nancy Thomas, "A Call for Academic Freedom," unpublished essay provided by the author, August 24, 2018.

6. On the protection of institutions, see, e.g., Timothy Snyder, *On Tyranny: Twenty Lessons from the Twentieth Century* (New York: Tim Duggan Books, 2017); Steven Levitsky and Daniel Ziblatt, *How Democracies Die*, 1st ed. (New York: Crown Publishing, 2018).

7. Amartya Sen, "Freedoms and Needs: An Argument for the Primacy of Political Rights," *New Republic* 210, nos. 2–3 (1994): 31–38.

8. John Villasenor, "Views among College Students Regarding the First Amendment: Results from a New Survey," https://www.brookings.edu/blog/fixgov/2017/09/18/views-among-college-students-regarding-the-first-amendment-results-from-a-new-survey/.

9. *Brandenburg v. Ohio*, 395 U.S. 444 (1969), https://supreme.justia.com/cases/federal/us/395/444/; *Watts v. United States*, 394 U. S. 705, see https://supreme.justia.com/cases/federal/us/394/705/case.html; Virginia v. Black, 2003, https://supreme.justia.com/cases/federal/us/538/343/case.html.

10. Erwin Chemerinsky and Howard Gillman, *Free Speech on Campus* (New Haven: Yale University Press, 2017).

11. Ibid., 14, 12.

12. I'm indebted to an essay by Archon Fung to help me sort out these issues. Archon Fung, "Campuses Never Had Completely Free Speech, Thank Goodness," unpublished essay provided by the author, October 8, 2017.

13. Ibid.

14. Dani Rodrik, "How Should Universities Handle the Trump Administration?," *Boston Globe*, BostonGlobe.com, https://www.bostonglobe.com/opinion/2018/08/12/how-should-universities-handle-trump-administration/O5B30Tf9CDovXhNkwjO6EL/story.html, accessed August 16, 2018.

15. Ibid.

16. My research argues that Yoo's torture memos contributed to the U.S. use of torture and that U.S. torture policy led to worsening torture in the forty countries that collaborated with the U.S. rendition program. See, e.g., Sikkink, *The Justice Cascade*, ch. 7, and Averell Schmidt and Kathryn Sikkink, "Partners in Crime: An Empirical Investigation of the CIA Rendition, Detention, and Interrogation Program," *Perspectives on Politics* 16, no. 4 (December 2018): 1014–33. Yoo has defended his actions in his book: John Yoo, *War by Other Means: An Insider's Account of the War on Terror* (New York: Atlantic Monthly Press, 2018).

17. On these topics, see Chemerinsky and Gillman, *Free Speech on Campus;* Martin Phillip Golding, *Free Speech on Campus* (Lanham, Md.: Rowman and Littlefield, 2000), Issues in Academic Ethics; and Sigal R.

Ben-Porath, *Free Speech on Campus* (Philadelphia: University of Pennsylvania Press, 2017).

18. *The Bell Curve* reports on racial differences in IQ scores in the United States but does not explore the reasons for these differences, thus tacitly condoning prejudice based on race. Eric Siegel, "The Real Problem with Charles Murray and 'The Bell Curve,'" *Scientific American* Blog Network, https://blogs.scientificamerican.com/voices/the-real-problem-with-charles-murray-and-the-bell-curve/, accessed August 16, 2018. Murray has responded to his critics in an interview with Frank Miele, in *Skeptic* 3, no. 2 (1995): 34–41, http://www.skeptic.com/archives24.html.

19. *New York Times*, March 13, 2017, https://www.nytimes.com/2017/03/13/opinion/understanding-the-angry-mob-that-gave-me-a-concussion.html, accessed July 24, 2018. See also "How the Middlebury Riot Really Went Down," *POLITICO Magazine*, https://www.politico.com/magazine/story/2017/05/28/how-donald-trump-caused-the-middlebury-melee-215195, accessed March 1, 2018.

20. Brandon Dixon and Anna Kuritzkes, "Charles Murray Even Draws Protest," *Harvard Crimson*, September 7, 2017, https://www.thecrimson.com/article/2017/9/7/charles-murray-visits-harvard/.

21. Https://www.thecrimson.com/article/2018/5/22/hks-diversity-free-speech/.

22. Villasenor, "Views among College Students Regarding the First Amendment."

23. Chemerinsky and Gillman, *Free Speech on Campus*, 10.

24. Erica Chenoweth and Maria J. Stephan, *Why Civil Resistance Works: The Strategic Logic of Nonviolent Conflict* (New York: Columbia University Press, 2011), Columbia Studies in Terrorism and Irregular Warfare.

25. Interview with Ramsey Champagne, community advocate, OSAPR, Cambridge, Ma., November 20, 2018.

26. Vanessa Grigoriadis, "I Spoke to 200 Students across America to Find Out Why Campus Rape Is So Prevalent," *Glamour*, https://www.glamour.com/story/why-is-campus-rape-still-so-prevalent, accessed August 16, 2018.

27. Zachary D. Kaufman, "Protectors of Predators or Prey: Bystanders and Upstanders amid Sexual Crimes," *Southern California Law Review* 92 (forthcoming).

28. Https://osapr.harvard.edu/pages/vocabulary.

29. Https://www.eventbrite.com/e/hollaback-bystander-interven tion-webinar-tickets-29417789400?utm-medium=discovery&utm campaign=social&utm-content=attendeeshare&aff=escb&utm source=cp&utm-term=listing.

30. Cheryl A. Thomas, "Legal Reform on Domestic Violence in Central and Eastern Europe and the Former Soviet Union," 14. Paper presented at U.N. Division for the Advancement of Women, Expert Group Meeting on Good Practices in Legislation on Violence against Women, Austria, May 26–28, 2008.

31. Zachary D. Kaufman, "Protectors of Predators or Prey: Bystanders and Upstanders amid Sexual Crimes," *Southern California Law Review* 92 (forthcoming). See also Zachary Kaufman, "When Sexual Abuse Is Common Knowledge—but Nobody Speaks Up," *Boston Globe*, BostonGlobe.com, https://www.bostonglobe.com/ ideas/2018/08/03/when-sexual-abuse-common-knowledge-but-nobody-speaks/bLoDyTfmKAO9yYxf1VE6zO/story.html, accessed August 17, 2018.

32. "Campus Sexual Violence: Statistics," RAINN, https://www. rainn.org/statistics/campus-sexual-violence, accessed July 25, 2018. In the case of the statistics listed in the source, they are drawing on David Cantor, Bonnie Fisher, Susan Chibnall, Reanna Townsend et. al., "Report on the AAU Campus Climate Survey on Sexual Assault and Sexual Misconduct," Association of American Universities, September 21, 2015.

33. Cantor et. al., "Report on the AAU Campus Climate Survey on Sexual Assault and Sexual Misconduct."

34. C. Krebs, C. Lindquist, T. Warner, B. Fisher, and S. Martin, "Campus Sexual Assault Study: Final Report, October 2007," https:// www.ncjrs.gov/pdffiles1/nij/grants/221153.pdf; Matthew Kimble, Andra-da Neacsiu et al., "Risk of Unwanted Sex for College Women: Evidence for a Red Zone," *Journal of American College Health*, 2008.

35. Joseph Shapiro, "Campus Sexual Assault Law Now Includes Language on Same Sex Violence," NPR, October 1, 2014, https://www. npr.org/2014/10/01/352757107/campus-sexual-assault-law-now-in cludes-language-on-same-sex-violence.

36. Https://pubs.niaaa.nih.gov/publications/CollegeFactSheet/ CollegeFactSheet.pdf.

37. Https://sapac.umich.edu/article/52.

38. David Lisak and Paul Miller, "Repeat Rape and Multiple Offending among Undetected Rapists," *Violence and Victims* 17, no. 1 (February 1, 2002): 73–84, https://doi.org/10.1891/vivi.17.1.73.33638. The reliability of this research has been questioned. See, for example, Linda LeFauve, "Campus Rape Expert Can't Answer Basic Questions about His Sources," *Reason*, July 28, 2005, https://reason.com/archives/2015/07/28/campus-rape-statistics-lisak-problem/.

39. Kevin M. Swartout et al., "Trajectory Analysis of the Campus Serial Rapist Assumption," *JAMA Pediatrics* 169, no. 12 (December 1, 2015): 1148–54, https://doi.org/10.1001/jamapediatrics.2015.0707.

40. Amelia Thomson-DeVeaux, "What If Most Campus Rapes Aren't Committed by Serial Rapists?," *FiveThirtyEight* (blog), July 13, 2015, quoting Kevin Swartout, https://fivethirtyeight.com/features/what-if-most-campus-rapes-arent-committed-by-serial-rapists/.

41. My thanks to Dara Cohen for drawing my attention to many of the issues and policy implications in this paragraph.

42. "Your Role in Preventing Sexual Assault," RAINN, https://www.rainn.org/articles/your-role-preventing-sexual-assault, accessed July 25, 2018.

43. C. A. Gidycz, L. M. Orchowski, and A. D. Berkowitz, "Preventing Sexual Aggression among College Men: An Evaluation of a Social Norms and Bystander Intervention Program," *Violence against Women* 17 (2011): 720–42.

44. Ibid.

45. Charlene Y. Senn et al., "Efficacy of a Sexual Assault Resistance Program for University Women," *New England Journal of Medicine* 372, no. 24 (June 11, 2015): 2326–35, https://doi.org/10.1056/NEJMsa1411131.

46. Grigoriadis, "I Spoke to 200 Students across America to Find Out Why Campus Rape Is So Prevalent." Grigoriadis interviewed Senn and noted she had a sign on her wall with these four rights listed.

47. Senn et al., "Efficacy of a Sexual Assault Resistance Program for University Women."

48. Ibid.

49. Ibid.

50. Quoted in "Sexual Assault Resistance Program for University Women Proves a Success," UToday, University of Calgary, June 12,

2015, https://www.ucalgary.ca/utoday/issue/2015–06–15/sexual-assault-resistance-program-university-women-proves-success.

51. Harvard University, Task Force on the Prevention of Sexual Assault, Final Report, March 7, 2016, 6.

52. Interview with Ramsey Champagne, community advocate, OSAPR, Cambridge, Ma., November 20, 2018.

Index

risk, 2, 5, 49, 69, 120, 139, 145; reduction, 140, 143, 146
Risse, Mathias, 20, 43
rivers, rights of, 11, 53
Roberts, David, 63–64, 74
Rodrik, Dani, 132, 135
Rotary Club, 75–76
Russia, 66, 70
Rwanda, 49

Saudi Arabia, 16, 66
Schulz, William, 33, 40
self-defense, 144–46
self-esteem, 95
self-interest, 8, 12, 18, 52, 112–15
Senn, Charlene, 144–46
sexual assault, 13–14, 25, 46, 125, 127, 137–48. *See also* #MeToo movement
Shell, 66
Shue, Henry, 19
Singapore: Clark, William, 58; Yew, Lee Kuan, 32
slavery, 15–16, 50
smart phones, 73, 122; privacy settings of, 8–9, 22
smoking, norms about, 17–18, 68, 112
social connection model, 25, 29, 44, 53–55, 65, 111, 126–28, 137, 147. *See also* networked responsibility
socialist thought, 27
specialized division of deliberate responsibility, 45, 48
speech. *See* free speech
stamp, 87, 90, 98, 100, 103
Stanger, Allison, 133, 137
Stephan, Maria, 137
Stone, Rebecca, 114
structural injustice, 11–12, 44, 65, 74
Sunlight Foundation, 87
survivor, 45, 138, 141–42, 147
Swanson, Ana, 64

technology companies. *See* Apple; Cambridge Analytica; Facebook; Google
Tennessee, 97
Thomas, Nancy, 86, 91
top 10 percent, 64
torture, 19, 36, 45, 132

trees, rights of, 11, 53
Trump: administration, 14, 50, 129, 132, 134–35; Donald, 19, 71–72, 121
Tufts University. 82, 84. *See also* Institute for Democracy and Higher Education; NSLVE; Thomas, Nancy
TurboVote, 86–91; Flaxman, Seth, 87; Kraft, Amanda Cassel, 87; Peters, Kathryn, 87

Uganda, 51
undergraduate students, 73, 84, 88–90, 92–94, 99, 106–7, 136, 141
United Nations General Assembly, 27, 34
United States: citizen, 87, 95, 102, 117; constitution, 13, 117; Supreme Court, 13, 102, 117, 130–31
Universal Declaration of Human Rights, 2, 27–29, 31–32, 34, 38
University of Minnesota, 100

Vaidhyanathan, Siva, 77
Victor, David G., 48
Vietnam War, 131
Virginia, 100
vote: responsibility to, 6, 14–15, 24, 79–81, 90–96, 103, 108, 114–19, 122; right not to, 110, 112, 116–18; right to, 6, 16, 24, 84, 105, 110, 116–17, 123
voter: mobilization, 103–4, 116, 122; registration, 88–91, 93, 99, 104, 111, 119 (*see also* National Voter Registration Day); suppression, 6, 98, 117, 119, 121; turnout, 79–87, 91–92, 101–3, 108–9, 115–16, 119, 123
voting: absentee, 90–91, 97–100, 107–8, 111; compulsory, 107, 121; irrationality of, 12, 113–16; student, 24, 86, 108–9, 114; youth, 84, 105, 108–9, 124

Wackenheim v. France. See dwarf-tossing
Waldron, Jeremy, 19